El Eternauta, Daytripper, and Beyond

World Comics and Graphic Nonfiction Series
Frederick Luis Aldama and Christopher Gonzalez, Editors
The World Comics and Graphic Nonfiction series includes monographs and edited volumes that focus on the analysis and interpretation of comic books and graphic nonfiction from around the world. The books published in the series use analytical approaches from literature, art history, cultural studies, communication studies, media studies, and film studies, among other fields, to help define the comics studies field at a time of great vitality and growth.

El Eternauta, Daytripper, and Beyond

Graphic Narrative in Argentina and Brazil

DAVID WILLIAM FOSTER

University of Texas Press   *Austin*

Chapter 1 is an expanded version of an essay published in *Transmodernity: Journal of Peripheral Cultural Production of the Luso-Hispanic World*, and it is used with the permission of the editors. Chapter 5 was originally published in *Critical Insights: Magical Realism* (ed. Ignacio López-Calvo), and it is used by permission of Salem Press/Grey House Publishing and the editor. Chapter 7 was originally published in *Ambitos Feministas*, and it is used with the permission of the editor.

Requests for permission to reproduce material from this work should be sent to:
Permissions
University of Texas Press
P.O. Box 7819
Austin, TX 78713-7819
http://utpress.utexas.edu/index.php/rp-form

⊗ The paper used in this book meets the minimum requirements of ANSI/NISO Z39.48-1992 (R1997) (Permanence of Paper).

Library of Congress Cataloging-in-Publication Data
Names: Foster, David William, author.
Title: El Eternauta, Daytripper, and beyond : graphic narrative in Argentina and
    Brazil / David William Foster.
Description: First edition. Austin : University of Texas Press, 2016. Includes
    bibliographical references and index.
Series: World comics and graphic nonfiction series
Identifiers: LCCN 2016012909 (print) LCCN 2016015679 (ebook)
    ISBN 9781477310847 (cloth : alk. paper)
    ISBN 9781477310854 (pbk. : alk. paper)
    ISBN 9781477310861 (library e-book)
    ISBN 9781477310878 (non-library e-book)
Subjects: LCSH: Comic books, strips, etc.—Argentina—History. Comic books,
    strips, etc.—Brazil—History. Graphic novels—Argentina—History and
    criticism. Graphic novels—Brazil—History and criticism.
Classification: LCC PN6790.A7 F67 2016 (print) LCC PN6790.A7 (ebook)
    DDC 741.5/982—dc23
    LC record available at https://LCCN.loc.gov/2016012909

10.7560/310847

To my students, as always.

Contents

    as Existential Journey   **106**

10. Women's Wondrous Power versus the Telluric Gods
    in Angélica Freitas and Odyr Bernardi's *Guadalupe*   **119**

    Notes   **129**

    Works Cited   **147**

    Index   **157**

Preface

Graphic narrative is understood to refer to a printed textual production in which a narrative is told through a combination of graphic images and literary text. On occasion images may predominate and the literary text may be a sort of sidebar commentary, dialogue balloons emanating from the mouths of characters, or a combination of the two. The term "graphic narrative" customarily implies a complex interaction between image and text intended to raise the aesthetic level of the graphic narrative beyond that of single-strip comics and longer comic-book stories oriented toward mass media readers. Although all of these genres may be interesting from the point of view of sociohistorical and ideological analysis, their relative transparency of meaning and the frequently "comic" nature of their stories have tended to keep them in a popular-culture category separate from the prestige literature that is the basic fare of academic critical study.

At issue is the distinction the Japanese make between *manga*, comic-book stories of passing or trivial interest, often characterized by recurring thematic and discursive conventions, and *gekiga* ("dramatic picture"), works considered more serious in intent and effect that engage the reader on multiple levels, characteristically with innovative thematic lines and discursive features. The transparency of artistic representation of the manga/comic book is typically replaced by the often abstract, expressionistic, and perceptually complex imagery of the *gekiga*/graphic novel.

The American Will Eisner is usually, if perhaps not accurately, credited with promoting the importance of graphic novels in the Japanese sense of *gekiga*, beginning with his work in the late 1970s. Focusing on themes, settings, and characters that were to be found in canonical fiction, Eisner modeled longer forms of graphic storytelling that required of the reader considerable attention to textual details and a sophisticated understanding of contemporary narrative paradigms. Moving between narrative extensions that appeared to be equivalent to long short stories or full novels, the graphic narrative evolved into self-contained, specifically titled publication units that vied for academic recognition and advanced critical analysis.[1]

While graphic novels may be adaptations of literary works (raising the bar on the older practice of "illustrated classics"), readers now look for original creative efforts. Art Spiegelman's two-volume narrative *Maus: A Survivor's Tale* (1986, 1991) is usually considered to have cemented the importance of the independently original graphic narrative in the United States. Not surprisingly, in addition to the awards Spiegelman has received for his novel, including the 1992 Pulitzer Prize Special Award, his work has been the subject of over a half-dozen book-length critical studies.[2] Graphic narratives are now a widely recognized separate publishing and library-collection development category.[3]

This monograph examines the development and major texts of graphic narrative in Argentina and Brazil, the two countries with the most extensive production in, respectively, Spanish and Portuguese.[4]

Since the concept of the graphic narrative as a unique cultural form is only about two decades old, much of the material, especially the texts examined from Argentina, involved the retroactive assignment of them to that category and their separation from the longer-standing genre of the comic book.[5] Precisely an example of such retroactively identified material will anchor the material examined here. I refer to the Argentine Héctor Germán Oesterheld's famous work *El Eternauta*, which was originally serialized 1957–1959. This is also the case with a long tradition of Argentine comic books and what one today would call the emergence of the graphic novel—in the midst of the larger comic-book production—in its appeal to more serious readers than fans of the ever-popular American materials (routinely translated in Argentina into Spanish) and their local imitators. Oesterheld, who prepared the written text, worked with a major graphic artist, Francisco Solano López. The material went on to receive such wide acclaim that the novel was revised in 1969 by Oesterheld and a sequel published in 1975.

After Oesterheld was "disappeared" by the neofascist military dictatorship that came to power in March 1976, the Eternauta figure was appropriated and reprised by diverse hands, such that it is now considered a venerable institution of Argentine culture. The original version by Oesterheld himself forms one of the most important cultural texts of the turbulent mid-twentieth century in Argentina, where, despite antedating the brutal military coup of 1976 that led to Oesterheld's disappearance and presumed murder during the so-called Dirty War against subversion, it is today routinely read as foretelling in a proleptic fashion the "invasion" of Argentine society by a murderous tyranny. Oesterheld may not have been disappeared because of *El Eternauta* (he became involved, along with his four daughters and their partners, in subversive activities), but his grim fate is directly connected in the Argentine imaginary with his famous novel.[6] Thus, as Oesterheld became committed to left-wing guerrilla movements in the 1970s, this and his other texts came to be invested heavily with significant sociohistorical dimensions that enhance their resonance with readers and are part of the privileged place *El Eternauta* holds in Argentine cultural production. Concomitantly, the sociohistorical dimensions of Oesterheld's work underscore the way in which, as far back as primitive graphic illustrations in nineteenth-century Argentina and important local "serious" comic books, this material was viewed as more analytical and engaged as cultural critique than the parallel Disney, DC Comics, Marvel, and Western Comics widely available in Spanish translation in the Argentine market. What all of this means is that the fame of *El Eternauta* and the by-now legendary aspects of Oesterheld's person have served to solidify in Argentina the uniqueness of graphic narrative in a way quite parallel to the similar role in the United States of Art Spiegelman's *Maus*.

The discussion of Oesterheld's major work will serve to introduce other important Argentine titles that will demonstrate the production in that country of a serious graphic novel tradition before the genre acquired cultural and critical recognition. Graphic narrative production in Argentina is extensive, almost as much as comic-book production had been in an earlier era, and perhaps because of *El Eternauta*'s privileged resonance, graphic narrative quickly emerged as a major platform for the culture of redemocratization of Argentina in the 1980s (the country officially returned to constitutional democracy in December 1983).[7] This, then, will be the basis of the Argentine materials examined here: a series of texts written against the backdrop of social and political issues that emerge from the dictatorship and cultural and critical assessments of it that began even before the official end in late 1983 of the military self-mandate. Not all of the material deals directly with Argentine thematic issues, nor does it all directly reference the 1976–1983 period of tyranny. However, because of the period of production and the importance of the artists involved—a veritable who's who of the genre in Argentina—the horizons of consciousness and awareness of the period are not difficult to profile. At the same time, the narratives with foreign settings—

for example, New York, in José Muñoz and Carlos Sampayo's *El Bar de Joe* (*Joe's Bar*)—exemplify the exile experience of these artists, like so many other Argentines, as a consequence of neofascist tyranny.

In the case of the Brazilian material, the focus is on a more recent production. Brazil, which returned to constitutional democracy in mid-1985 after a long-running dictatorship (1964–1985) with rising and falling periods of authoritarianism but little of the overt neofascism Argentina experienced, produced little in the way, after 1985, of the sort of highly defined analysis of the period of repression Argentina did.[8] As a result, although comic-book production remains high, as did the production of high-quality graphic adaptations of major Brazilian literary works, it has only been in the past two decades that a strong inventory of Brazilian graphic narratives has emerged. These narratives show little interest in dealing with the sociopolitical issues of dictatorship and redemocratization in Brazil. Rather, they are very much tied to the aggressive culture of modernity that has characterized Brazil in recent decades, a culture that is ever attuned to matters of internationalism, globalization, and cross-cultural identity, especially where English and American life are involved.

It is therefore no surprise that the Brazilian material examined, even when it was not written directly in English, as Fábio Moon and Gabriel Bá's coauthored works now are, shows a high-level consciousness of English, as in the case of Rafael Grampá's *Mesmo Delivery*, which is the title of both the Portuguese original and the English translation. And although Angélica Freitas, with her novel *Guadalupe*, is not the first Latin American graphic artist to set her story abroad, there is a sense of Mexican society and the Spanish language that runs deep in her work. By contrast, the Argentines José Muñoz and Carlos Sampayo's *El Bar de Joe* is set in New York but without any real sense of the city: it could well be any of thousands of bars in Buenos Aires as regards existential themes and social issues.[9] The result is a group of texts that very much represents the nature and quality of life today in Brazil, correlating on an artistic level with the economic and political horizons afforded by Brazil's prominence as a member of the so-called BRICS countries of greatest emerging internationalist development. Because of this contemporaneity, this is an ongoing production, and I could well have included a half-dozen other texts that have been published in the past few years.

My specific goal has been to read the texts in semiotic and ideological terms in the attempt to understand narrative design and sociopolitical significance within the respective parameters for Argentina and Brazil.[10] That is, while I am interested in the artistic practices underlying the generation and structure of texts that articulate interpretations of individual and collective lives, I will be particularly concerned with how those interpretations are ideologically circumscribed by social, political, and historical forces that configure Latin American reading publics. Literature is most assuredly viewed in Latin America as predominantly an intervention in public debates over ideological practices of institutions, governments, artists, and citizens as part of their daily lives. While one would not want to overly monumentalize Oesterheld, his disappearance and presumed death at the hands of the military dictatorship attests to the way in which his graphic narratives struck very serious chords in Argentina in the 1970s and why they have been crucial to the cultural production of post-1983 redemocratization. In general, my analytical approach to Latin American graphic narrative parallels my extensive published research on other manifestations of visual arts in Latin America, such as the popular comic, photography, and narrative and documentary filmmaking.

There is also a second and unifying dimension to this study, which is the focus on linguistics issues. My interest does not lie in attempting to tease out particular linguistic registers for Argentine or Brazilian graphic novels. Rather, an attention to the materiality of language is one of the major parameters of my research on cultural production, and I find myself continually drawn to how specific linguistic features intersect with semiotic and ideological dimensions of cultural texts. Such issues need to be drawn together eventually as a major topic of critical inquiry, but that remains the subject of monograph to be undertaken at some future time.

In addition to the support of the teaching and research programs of Arizona State University, this project has enjoyed the technical and academic support of many individuals. Technical assistance has been provided by Joseph Desamais. Academic support has been provided by colleagues and research associates: Daniel Holcombe, Jorge Gimeno Robles, José Juan Gómez Becerra, Andrés Ruiz Olaya, Élida B. Messina, Enrique Medina, Diego Kenis, Charles St-Georges, Patrick Ridge, Amanda Mollindo. My special thanks, as always, to Patricia Hopkins, my first reader in English, who never lets me forget that sentences usually have main verbs.

Note: In providing translations for quotes, I have included brief translations in brackets within the text; longer ones are footnoted.

El Eternauta, Daytripper, and Beyond

ARGENTINA AND THE FORGING OF A TRADITION OF GRAPHIC NARRATIVE: MILITARY TYRANNY AND REDEMOCRATIZATION

CHAPTER 1

Masculinity as Privileged Human Agency in H. G. Oesterheld's *El Eternauta*

La inocente lectura de 1957 dejó de ser posible (después del golpe militar de 1976). El Eternauta ya no era más una conmovedora historia de ciencia ficción; se parecía demasiado a una antigua profecía de lo que estaba pasando en el mundo real. La más grande de las historietas argentinas regresaba, esquivando censores, para ser leída como un himno a la libertad, a la necesidad de pelear contra los monstruos, a que la vida es lo más importante que hay sobre la Tierra . . . En fin, cada tiempo parece permitir sacar de estas páginas una lectura diferente.
[The innocent reading of 1957 became no longer possible (after the 1976 military coup). El Eternauta was no longer a moving science-fiction story; it came close to an ancient prophecy of what was going on in the real world. Argentina's greatest comic strip came back, sidestepping the censors, to be read as a hymn to liberty, to the need to fight against monsters because life is the most important thing on the face of the Earth. (. . .) In the end, every time period seems to allow for deriving a different reading from these pages.]
CARLOS TRILLO, 12−13

El Eternauta (first published serially in 1957–1959), with narrative by Héctor Germán Oesterheld (1919–1978) and drawings by Francisco Solano López (1928–2011), is perhaps the most beloved and even revered of Argentine cultural texts.[1] Other works of national culture—such as José Hernández's narrative poem on Gaucho life, the *Martín Fierro* (*Ida* [1872; the title *Ida* is a reading convention], *Vuelta* [1879]),[2] the poetry and lyrics of the much-vaunted Argentine tango, or even Julio Cortázar's boom novel *Rayuela* (1963)—are widely honored for distilling the essence of the Argentine character. But in terms of near veneration, the

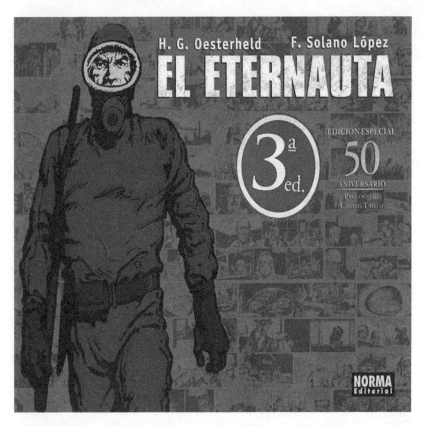

H. G. Oesterheld and F. Solano López, *El Eternauta*

Oesterheld–Solano López graphic novel not only tapped into rich veins of the national imaginary, but for sheer originality it continues to stand unrivaled in Latin American graphic narrative production.[3]

I would like in this chapter to explore the role of masculinity in *El Eternauta* and how the preeminence of masculinity is related to the sense of Argentine society Oesterheld maintained and the privilege of masculine responsibility and accomplishment. I will explore (1) the masculine world of the story itself; (2) the significance of the story as it relates to Oesterheld's own personal role in the political turmoil of the late 1970s and his own disappearance at the hands of the military dictatorship; (3) the androcentrism of *El Eternauta*; (4) the importance of men as agents of social change; (5) the use of the *tú* form in the novel as a marker of masculine transcendence; and (6) the social commitment of the male narrator.[4]

The Story

The framing of the narrative world in *El Eternauta* is unmistakably masculinist: Juan Salvo, the Argentine Everyman, aided by a small group of
male friends, attempts to save his world, paragonized in terms of his wife
and young daughter.[5] The gender disjunction could not be more stark.
With a given name that is the most common male name in Spanish and
a surname (likely Italo-Argentine) that evokes the verb *salvar*, "to save,"
Salvo is the *salvador*, the "savior."[6] The way in which Juan Salvo is, ultimately, an ineffective Everyman for a successful savior is what makes
Oesterheld's narrative interesting. Indeed, if read (or if, after 1976, it is
inevitable that it be read) as an allegory of imperialist interventionism
and military regimes in Argentina in the twentieth century, the foreign
interventions they defended and the resistance by sectors of the ordinary
citizenry to them,[7] *El Eternauta* cannot help but confirm the inefficacy
of resistance to the alien invaders, and Juan Salvo's disappearance into
the time continuum, as I have already noted, eerily foreshadows Oesterheld's own disappearance, his remains (so far) unaccounted for, at the
hands of the agents of state repression.

El Eternauta begins humbly enough, both in terms of the general
setting of the story and the tale itself. Although so-called local-color
comic strips were often set in Buenos Aires, anything that counted as a
serious story followed the lead of foreign imports in being set in paradigmatic international locales such as New York or London. As Carlos
Trillo points out in his introduction to what is considered the definitive
edition of *El Eternauta*, part of the attraction of Oesterheld's narrative
from the outset was its setting in a Buenos Aires that, despite what will
be the science-fiction format, beginning with the contaminated ash falling over the city, was immediately familiar to readers, down to political
slogans of the day (9).

But what is most affectively engaging about the framing of *El Eternauta*, what makes its humble narrative setting so viscerally recognizable
for the Argentine reader, is the way in which the narrative begins with a
story within a story that involves the crucial reduplication of, literally, a
homey residential setting. Moreover, this republication is tied together
by a significant detail of difference between the interrelated stories. *El
Eternauta* is framed initially by a first-person narrative in which the artist's alter ego is occupied, one chilly winter night in the wee hours, in
writing one of the scripts for a graphic narrative. He occupies a comfortable study in a comfortable stand-alone house (what in Argentina is

called a *chalet*) in one of the series of agreeable bedroom communities that extend northwest up the Río de la Plata delta from Buenos Aires.

Suddenly the narrator sees materialize in the chair in front of his desk the figure of the man we will learn is the Eternauta, who has been traveling through time on an eternal quest. He informs the narrator that he needs to have a place to rest for a while before continuing on his journey. Despite his wan appearance and his strange futuristic clothing, the narrator is sympathetic to him, but reluctant to accommodate him. Juan, as the stranger has identified himself, undertakes to tell his story, confident, he says, that it will convince the narrator to honor his request for refuge. The graphic novel we read subsequently is Juan's story.

Juan's story also begins in a comfortable chalet in an agreeable bedroom community, this time explicitly identified as Vicente López. It is also late at night, although not quite as late as in the outer narrative. Juan is engaged in playing a game of *truco* (an Argentine equivalent of poker) with three close male friends and associates, in the attic of the house, while his wife Elena reads in bed downstairs and Martita, his young daughter, sleeps safely in her bed, clutching her toy bunny. The radio is on, and a news bulletin announces that an atomic test by the Americans in the South Pacific has released a flurry of radioactive contamination that is moving west across the globe. Only minutes later the quiet of the night is interrupted by the sound of colliding vehicles. As the friends rush to the window they see a sort of snow, glowing radioactively, falling on the city. Contact with it seems to kill almost instantly, and they deduce that anyone exposed directly to it has died or will soon die. They have been saved because, thanks to the extra chill of the evening, Juan's well-insulated house has been tightly closed against the outside air.

The group directly witnesses the toxic effects of the snowfall when one of the card players, hysterical over the fate of his family, suddenly rushes out the front door, which is fortunately slammed in time to keep any of the radioactive drifts from entering the house. They watch him through the window quickly fall victim to the contamination blanketing the city. The narrative that follows after this point will deal with Juan's, his family's, and his friends' attempts at survival and their confrontation with an alien force that arrives with the toxic cloud (which we subsequently learn did not come from the American bomb blast). In this sense, the narrative will be built as an example of action comics and the survivalist motif, around the advances and reversals, the obstacles and overcoming them, to what is the obsessive and focused concern of the survivors: to continue living. I will discuss below how this undertaking is carried out and how Oesterheld entertains a double happy ending for his narrative, one that corresponds to both outer and inner stories.

I noted that there was a significant difference, however, between these stories that affects the way in which they are linked together as reduplicating settings. This difference involves the window: first the window in the narrator's study and then the window in Juan's attic workshop/laboratory where the four men are playing cards. In the outer narrative, the man who writes scripts for graphic narratives—i.e., Oesterheld—has left his window open to admit the bracing drafts of the three a.m. nighttime air, which is what the writer prefers as he works. Hearing a noise he cannot place, something like a slight movement in the armchair in front of his desk, he looks up at the Eternauta, seeking a place to rest before resuming the search through time for his family. As the writer balks, Juan Salvo launches into the long narrative that is the actual graphic novel. The open window signals invitation (more figurative than literal) for the writer's inspirations; as we'll see in a moment, the window does, in fact, become the inspiration for what the reader reads, *El Eternauta*, the mediated version of Salvo's story.

In the inner story, by contrast, it is the closed, virtually hermetically sealed window that is the occasion of the escape of the Salvo family and their truco-playing guests from the deadly ash that suddenly begins to blanket Buenos Aires and its suburbs. One of Oesterheld's conceits is that virtually no one is saved from whatever it is in the ash that kills people almost instantly: in addition to people on the street, individuals succumb because they leave windows open, if ever so slightly, despite the cold winter night.[8] Since apparently most residents of Buenos Aires are not afraid of the night air, they are felled in their sleep or in their armchairs by the ash, or, if they have their windows closed, they become victims when they rush to see the unheard-of meteorological phenomenon, throwing wide their windows in the process. At least in terms of the radius of operations of Salvo, his friends, and eventual ad hoc crusaders against the invaders—a swath of the city extending from the Vicente López suburb down through the mostly well-to-do neighborhoods on the city's north rim and into the central plaza of Government House— virtually no one else has been saved.

Much has been made of the heroic nature of Salvo and his two close associates, Favalli, who teaches physics at the university (one of the four truco players), and the younger Franco (he addresses Salvo and Favalli always with the formal *usted* form), called El Tornero (lathe operator) since this is, in fact, his occupation at a factory. Their heroism derives from the sense of the abiding dignity of human life, which must be protected against the unknown invading forces; in the sense of the beauty of their world that is under threat and must be preserved; in their commitment to a solidarity of humankind, which is threatened by the breakdown of society and the potential for the emergence of the law of the jungle; in their commitment to each other, either as a longtime friend (Favalli) or as a new friend (Franco), whose manifest youthful, manly values signal to the older men that he is unquestionably one of them; in the courage with which they confront the ever-shifting face of the invader, which is represented by something like a hierarchy of forces of aggression whose superior technical range is only challenged by the human ingenuity and moral grounding of Salvo and his associates; and in their willingness to soldier on despite the many setbacks and losses they suffer. Indeed, one of the recurring motifs of the story is the cry ". . . Esto sí que es el final" ([This is really the end] 218), uttered in this case by Salvo, although the others seem to take turns in proclaiming their finish and the destruction of humankind and the terrestrial world as they know it.

A large measure of the resonance of *El Eternauta* has to do with how external details of the text relate to the dark history of authoritarian and neofascist tyranny in Argentina throughout much of the twentieth century, especially in the crucial 1966–1983 period in which the country experienced state-sponsored terror at the hands of recurrent military regimes.[9] The story of *El Eternauta* and Oesterheld's personal biography have become so intimately linked that, despite the enormous importance of the graphic representation of Oesterheld's text achieved by Francisco Solano López, one of Argentina's most outstanding graphic artists, *El Eternauta*, as a cultural text, is often evoked exclusively with reference to Oesterheld.[10]

Three separate versions of *El Eternauta* are customarily recognized (see Muñoz for a detailed account of the various editions of the narrative). The first, the 1957–1959 publication in the magazine *Hora cero*, corresponds with the so-called Revolución Libertadora that deposed Juan Domingo Perón in 1955, inaugurating a series of repressive military regimes that will culminate in the neofascist tyranny of 1976–1983. Oesterheld undertook a 1969 remake of the narrative in 1968, turning to the equally talented Alberto Breccia (1919–1993) for the illustrations; this is the period of the sequence of military regimes known as the Revolución Argentina, three regimes that sought to suppress popular political movements but that saw the emergence of intense guerrilla opposition to their de facto power. Finally, Oesterheld prepared a sequel to *El Eternauta*, again with Solano López executing the graphic accompaniment, in 1975, on the eve of the Proceso de Reconstrucción Nacional. In 1976 the military attributed to itself the unimpeachable right to eliminate extrajudicially any and all opposition, active or passive, to its ideology of a new Argentine national state.[11] Oesterheld's remake of *El Eternauta* in 1969, usually gauged in terms of the increased direct reference in the text to the military regime and its foreign supporters (other Latin American military regimes and various US administrations), corresponded with his own personal direct involvement in armed guerrilla activity with his entrance into the Montonero nationalist-leftist movement, a commitment that he shared with all four of his daughters.

Oesterheld and the 1976 Military Coup

Oesterheld disappeared at the hands of state repression in 1977 and is presumed to have died in 1978; his four daughters disappeared between 1976 and 1977.[12] It is the emotional impact of this fate for the author and all four of his daughters that accounts to a large degree for the association of the graphic narrative with the author of its text alone. Oesterheld inserted himself increasingly into the text of the remake as a character-witness of events. With his disappearance (his remains have never been located) one can say that he suffered a fate akin to that of his character. El Eternauta's name refers to how—through an error in handling the instruments of a space ship that produces his separation from his family, which he is trying to save—Juan becomes lost in the time continuum, seeking eternally his lost wife and daughter.

El Eternauta enjoys privileged status in the history of Argentine graphic narrative, which extends back to the nineteenth century through a rich tradition of comic-book narrative that produced many offshoots in terms of the extended and imaginatively complex formats that we have come to identify as contemporary graphic narrative and treat as a distinct cultural genre. Its stature is a consequence of the way in which Oesterheld insisted, in a way consonant with his political convictions, on his main character as a collective or group hero,[13] thereby emphatically contrasting him with the recurring Western convention of solitary action superheroes, whether by virtue of extraterrestrial forces (Superman) or intensely personally cultivated commitments (the Lone Ranger). Indeed, the influence of the solitary superhero in Argentina was two-fold

and therefore extensively subscribed to by the local industry. Such influence came first in the form of the many translations into Spanish of
American and European (today, one would include Japanese) publications and second in terms of the way in which creations by Argentine
artists adhered to those foreign models, often down to the names of the
characters. Whereas an Argentine artist like Roberto Fontanarrosa will
satirize this practice in his internationally famous *Boogie, el aceitoso* (first
created in 1972 and published until sometime in the 1990s; the name
refers to the Humphrey Bogart paradigm of the hardboiled detective),
Oesterheld, less committed than Fontanarrosa to the outrageously hu-
morous, views his title character as a complex human subject deeply enmeshed, mostly against his will (at least initially), in the Argentine sociopolitical history of the mid-twentieth century.[14]

Most importantly, *El Eternauta* has engaged readers because of its ingenious use of the framework of science fiction.[15] Although in the end,
Oesterheld could not escape the attention of the apparatus of repression
in Argentina in the late 1970s, it appears to have been for his overt political involvement with the Montoneros and not for his graphic novel.[16]
In other cases, artists were disappeared primarily for their creative works
and not for direct political activity, as was the case with Haroldo Conti,
whose writing had won an important literary prize in Cuba, and the film
director Raymundo Gleyzer, who did the first substantive television reporting in Argentina on the Cuban Revolution. Rodolfo Walsh, whose
writings were suspect, like Oesterheld was an early victim of repression
for his organizational role in the Montoneros.

Yet it was clear that artists could hardly provide unmediated, transparent representations of what was happening in Argentina. This was increasingly so as events moved forward from the military-imposed end
of Perón's presidency in 1955, particularly in the period after the military coup of 1976. None of the commitments of the period to documentary realism and contestatory postures, whether in the form of testimo-
nial writing or specifically nonnarrative documentary filmmaking, were
viable options. Even in cases where authors availed themselves of para-
ble, allegory, or even fantasy, censorship had become a semiotic undertaking, the censors highly skilled in finding objectionable content, with
consequences that were hardly ambiguous.[17] *El Eternauta*, while the
general visible contours of Buenos Aires and its daily life[18] are those of
the "present moment" of the narratives' successive installments, makes
use of the tropes of science fiction:[19] alien invasion, sophisticated technological equipment, and unusual events (such as the snowfall-like radioactive ash over a city whose weather normally excludes any snowfall).

H. G. Oesterheld and F. Solano López, *El Eternauta*

Also pertinent is the disjunction between the nefarious agents of Evil and the simple Everyman represented by the hero, Juan Salvo, drawn against his will into a drama almost beyond his understanding only because he is convinced that he is called upon to protect his family and a meaningful way of life that cannot be simply given up to the invading forces without a struggle. At issue is the extent to which, overlooking certain details and perhaps forcing a certain interpretation, these narrative details can be read as an allegory of a national way of life, held in sacred trust by every sane and well-intentioned citizen, threatened by superior evil extramural forces, and specifically as a question of resistance to the complicity of the internal agents of the invading forces. When Salvo and his men capture one of the Manos, the human-like agents of the unseen evil Ellos, it is Salvo who reminds them of the world whose way of life they are defending.

It is also eventually, especially after 1976, a meaning that reflects an understanding during the period of the interventionist influence of the United States on military tyranny and the degree to which the military dictatorship, with its strategies of exploitation and procedures of state terror, was primarily doing the bidding of forces with little interest in the preservation of the daily life of the Argentine Everyman; rather, quite the contrary—all aspects of local culture were to be sacrificed to the enhancement of alien interests. The monumentalization of *El Eternauta* occurred in part because of the way in which this bare narrative outline indexed as much for the overthrow of Perón (the mid-1950s) as for the defense of foreign interests and their local agents during the period of transnationalism opposed by guerrilla movements (the mid-1970s) and the neofascist process of the reconstruction of the national state following the ruthless destruction of all forms of opposition (the period following the 1976 coup). Where this can be particularly discerned in the narrative is not in the direct association of invading forces with Yankee imperialism or that of European allies, but in the way in which the "northern" societies are willing to take Buenos Aires out with an atomic bomb in order to annihilate the extraterrestrial evil before it attacks the north. The proposition that Buenos Aires or anywhere else in the so-called Third World is expendable in the defense of northern civilizations is particularly troubling.[20]

The Androcentrism of *El Eternauta*

Only a minimal reading of graphic narratives is enough for one to grasp the way in which they are essentially androcentric, no less so in Argentina. Indeed, in Argentina, cultural production is so resolutely androcentric that, while it has generated perhaps the most abundant feminist cultural production in Latin America as a response, it is still difficult to speak of recognized works and figures prior to the latter third of the twentieth century that are not male-identified.[21] Argentine tango lyrics are androcentric; women are virtually absent from the *Martín Fierro*, except as a literary pretext; Borges's extensive oeuvre is, with the limited exception of some memorable women, notably free of female characters, although he does occasionally, very occasionally, speak of some women authors (he was one of Virginia Woolf's Spanish-language translators).[22]

The history of Argentine comic books turns on male characters, and this carries over into graphic fiction.[23] To be sure, Salvador Joaquín Lavado's cartoon strip *Mafalda* (drawn between the early 1960s and 1973 under the pen name Quino) is an outstanding exception, with its beloved young heroine. This most famous figure in Latin American graphic humor stood virtually alone in the field as an exponent of a female-marked outlook on her society until the work of Maitena Burundarena (1962–), known mostly as simply Maitena, whose work dates from 1993. Maitena focuses on women of all ages—indeed, on women who experience the arc of chronological life—and her acerbic humor exemplifies very effectively the often strident feminism of recent decades, along with frequently hilarious representations of the self-doubts and internal contradictions of diverse feminist commitments (see scholarship on Maitena by Breckenridge, Pérez, and Tompkins).

Oesterheld's work, then, was no exception to this general pattern and, save for the text he devoted to Eva Perón, drawn by Alberto Breccia, there are no female characters of note in his work. In the case of *El Eternauta*, the male-male adversarial relationship that is the core of the story is certainly understandable. Societal power is in the hands of men, whether they be the forces of Evil (repressive governments, hostile aliens, or the internal agents of the latter—who are also the leaders of the former) or the forces of Good (the resistance on the part of the band of friends in *El Eternauta* or the organized guerrilla opposition in which Oesterheld and his daughters came to participate).[24]

The Importance of Men as Social Agents

Oesterheld's artistic strategy is to cast—against the drumbeat of apocalyptic utterance—the iterated representation of his male character's ability to confront overwhelming danger, to counter it and pull through, and regroup for the next challenge. While the narrative is punctured by the men's equally iterated moments of misplaced euphoria over having defeated the enemy, these rhetorical formulas serve as sort of a verbal skeleton for the narrative's displays of their prowess that is, in the final instance, based on the essential humanity of the individual working in efficient concert with the essential humanity of others. When the manly facade—i.e., the display of essential humanity that is manifest in the manly facade—breaks down (moments of terror and panic, moments of hallucination induced by the enemy, moments of profound self-doubt), it only serves as a transitory narrative reversal that quickly becomes corrected by the restoration of the facade and the movement forward of what, in affective terms, is the expected, customary flow of events in an action narrative.

This is, then, an action narrative such as the horizons of narrative meaning of the day would demand of Argentine literature and action comics would. It is a world of men battling mostly unknown forces of evil to save the world and the planet (exemplified by the loved ones, which, in this case mean Salvo's wife Elena and their little daughter, Martita). This does not necessarily mean that Good will triumph. It is enough for Evil to be evaded, as is the case when Salvo commandeers an abandoned spaceship only, in his lack of familiarity with its mechanism, to launch his wife and daughter into another time continuum from the one into which he launches himself. There is a happy ending to this story, but I will return to that in a moment.

What is significant to underscore here is that the struggle against Evil in all of the manifestations that give narrative substance to *El Eternauta* can only be executed by male characters. Indeed, aside from the wife and daughter, who are both bystanders and the motivating source of the narrative (in the sense that they symbolize why and for what the world must be saved: the promise of the heterosexual matrimonial unit and its legitimate and life-renewing offspring), there is only one other woman in *El Eternauta*, and she turns out to be a survivor who has been transformed into a robot, one of the hierarchy of agents of Evil in the narrative. Appropriately seductive in a catsuit and the unblemished visage of a starlet, she distracts Franco, who seems to have become a bit needy for opposite-sex company no matter how firm his homosocial bonds to Salvo and Favalli are. But the latter prevail, and Franco suddenly shoots the siren dead, realizing that she has been sent to dupe them and lure them into a trap.

It is never made clear in *El Eternauta* what the invading aliens are after and why they have chosen Buenos Aires as their point of entry into Earth. Although rarely directly articulated, in conventional science fiction the so-called First World is often the site of entry, whether—in addition to European capitals, New York, Los Angeles, Washington, or Chicago—there are examples of arrival at some remote locale. The reader assumes it is for the wealth of the First World, for the threat to alien planets of the scientific and technical aspirations of Earth, or for the potential dangers those aspirations, particularly when ill-conceived, may bring: aliens, just like illegal immigrants, may invade us because we have something they need or want, or we may be invaded because our folly is a threat to what the aliens have and do not want to lose. Alternatively, the aliens want to talk to people in charge of Earth and therefore go directly to the centers of power, demanding to be taken to the Earthlings' leader. Other narrative primes may be involved, but these two are strong pretexts. Yet, in neither of these two cases or potential others is it ever made clear why Ellos wish to disrupt the echt-domestic truco game of Juan Salvo and his closest friends.

Since it is a man's world that is being challenged, that of the truco players (Elena reads peacefully in bed, while Martita sleeps the sleep of the innocent with her stuffed bunny), it is the men who must save it. The weaker may fall by the wayside (two of the truco partners are felled early on), but the two stronger men of the four are able to forge an unbreakable bond and to bring others into their tight-knit unit to do valiant battle over and over against the enemy. One is confident in venturing the opinion that Oesterheld's public could find no grounds to reproach the manliness of these warriors and that the unspoken, probably mostly unconscious, desire of predominantly male readers to enter into this homosocial inner circle is one element that accounts for the enormous success of *El Eternauta* at the time of its original publication and its continuing favor with Argentine and Latin American reading audiences. Even after Oesterheld's disappearance at the hands of the equally masculinist but decidedly nefarious military regime, there was interest in continuing the series, although, ultimately, with little commercial or critical success.

Tú as a Marker of Masculine Transcendence

One of the most curious dimensions of *El Eternauta*, one that perhaps might be explained in terms of the mythified masculinity it represents, is the writer's decision to use the non-Argentine *tú* form of familiar address.[25] Oesterheld's characters are all Argentine (except for the agents of the invading forces, who mysteriously speak perfect Spanish), and while their speech is not assertively colloquial, they speak like Argentines, in both everyday words (e.g., *vereda* [sidewalk]) and slang (e.g., *chambón* [bumpkin]). The setting is clearly Buenos Aires, with all of the details of urban setting and life in place, including the details mentioned above of political and advertising slogans. It is the Buenos Aires of a certain level of middle-class prosperity (hence, the bedroom-community chalet that Salvo and his family occupy) in the late 1950s, a Buenos Aires that is on the cusp of the globalization that will come in subsequent decades of both military and democratic rule.

Buenos Aires is decidedly better off than its nearby urban capitals, like Santiago or Montevideo, and much better off than the outer ring of La Paz, Asunción, and Lima. But Buenos Aires is neither New York nor is it Los Angeles, and only a nationalistic criterion of narrative art can satisfy the challenge as to why Buenos Aires. Yet Oesterheld chooses to have his characters speak as though they were residents of Mexico City or Madrid, something (if one could be allowed some rhetorical exaggeration) like having the characters in a Superman action story using the *thou* form. One wonders if Oesterheld intended some sort of gesture toward a mythical realm of human conduct beyond the down-and-dirty everyday world of prevailing colloquial norms with which the Argentine *vos* is unquestionably associated. Everyday men may well be associated with the use of colloquial language and slang, but social avatars are held to a higher linguistic standard.

A veritable objective correlative of the gritty urban texture of Porteño (i.e., port resident) life, of the dank spaces that prevail in the city, of the sewer vapors that suddenly appear to give the city its signature fragrance, the *vos* is as inseparable from Buenos Aires as the so-called Brooklyn twang is from New York, even when the former is more universally prevalent than the latter as a linguistic metonym of the respective cities. Surely, Oesterheld could not have thought he was "universalizing" his narrative, any more than Quino would have supposedly universalized *Mafalda* by having her speak using the *tú* form.[26] By the late 1950s, Argentine literature is being written exclusively with the *vos*, Roberto Arlt's *Los siete locos* (1929) having set (not always with complete success) the tone for this authentic morphological feature of Argentine Spanish,[27] and it is really quite inconceivable that, by 1960, any serious Argentine writer would wish to hold onto the *tú* form of familiar address for, at least, Argentine characters.[28] Thus, one finds quite notable Oesterheld's preference for the *tú* form in a narrative that is so quintessentially Argentine and where the virtues of Argentine manhood are so prominently on display, as they are repeatedly tested and sometimes triumph quite noticeably against extraterrestrial forces that are basically summarized as pure Evil. As a privileged note of male-male bonding, perhaps perceivable as more abstract and idealized than would be the case with the scrappily quotidian *vos*, the *tú* form in *El Eternauta* stands out as a counterpart of masculinist prevalence.

H. G. Oesterheld and F. Solano López, *El Eternauta*

The Social Commitment of the Male Narrator

If the window brings together the inner and the outer narratives of *El Eternauta*, a secondary instance of male-male bonding also occurs here, and it serves to give *El Eternauta* a particularly satisfying *envoi* beyond the conventional one of earthly masculinity triumphant over extraterrestrial Evil. Indeed, it remains open whether extraterrestrial Evil can be defeated. As Salvo concludes his narrative, which has forged something like a bond between him and the writer of graphic narratives whose home he has "invaded" through the open window, the two men come to a startling conclusion: Salvo has been describing events that took place in 1963, while at that moment in the writer's study it is 1959, corresponding with the year in which *El Eternauta* concludes as a serial text. Salvo quickly understands that he has not been telling a tale of past events but engaging in the proleptic act of telling a story that will unfold in the future on the basis of the circumstances of 1959. Realizing that

H. G. Oesterheld and F. Solano López, *El Eternauta*

he can find his wife and daughter at home around the corner, he rushes out of the writer's house and morphs back into the Salvo of 1959, who (lovely hoary cliché) simply went out for the evening newspaper and was delayed a bit. Although Elena and Marta were beginning to get a bit worried, equilibrium is restored when Salvo's truco partners show up for their nightly game; Salvo has forgotten all about the events of the past-future and the routine daily Porteño life has rescued him from the time continuum in which he was lost.

In this fashion, *El Eternauta* enters the realm of those science-fiction tales that tell a cautionary tale of what might or could happen if human-kind does not change its ways. As Oesterheld's double is left trying to sort out what he has heard and what has just happened—Salvo no longer even knows who he is, since he has been so miraculously restored to the present moment of 1959—he wonders if, perhaps, turning it into one of his own narratives might just serve to prevent so much horror from coming to pass. This is a thoroughly delightful and satisfactory conclusion for the Eternauta's story, one that avoids either a conclusive end-of-the-world scenario (always unsatisfying to action narrative readers because their heroes do not triumph) or a conclusive win by the heroes (something readers appreciate, even if it is predictable both as regards the qualities of the heroes and their privileged historical extraction—i.e., paradigmatically European white men). While Oesterheld's triumvirate might be satisfactory proxies for a US-style Superman triumph over the forces of Evil, it would make *El Eternauta* just another example of action narrative formulas. By proposing a metanarrative ending for the story, it leaves open whether Buenos Aires will really be the site of the terrestrial Armageddon. And in the process, it proposes a masculinist supplement to Salvo's story: the pact between men that propels the narrative bulk of *El Eternauta* has now become a pact between Salvo and the writer. It is a pact whereby the writer's privilege in having heard Salvo's story—driven by Salvo's willingness to share his story with another man whose life is so similar to his own, down to the detail that they live around the corner from each other—will become the privilege of writing it up as the novel *El Eternauta* that we, in necessary complicity with this world of men (if we weren't, we wouldn't accept the premises of the narrative), will read and understand as the potential 1963 foretold in the 1959 of that narrative that will not come to pass. Thus, this "back-to-the-future" narrative acquires a metanarrative level that helps to cement its own masculinist privilege in Argentine cultural production.

Although I began by referring to the fame of *El Eternauta* as driven in large measure by the possibility of an allegorical reading (an allegorical reading, admittedly, more present in the Oesterheld-Breccia 1969 remake that never gained definitive traction with readers or critics, provoking instead much protest [Hojman Conde 143]), it should be clear that I am not advocating an allegorical reading for *El Eternauta*. Not only do many of the actual narrative details make this difficult, but *El Eternauta* was really conceived and written during a period of shaky political tranquility but with a measure of socioeconomic stability. It was a period between the Peronista period and the subsequent military dictatorship and the renewed military dictatorship of the 1960s during which the real campaign from the leftover American intervention, the transnational onslaught, and the betrayal of the people and the working class actually began to be part of the national cultural discourse.[29] Although political stability could be sketchy during the period, it was a far cry from what would take place during the 1970s which, until the 1976 military coup, was the apex of left-wing guerrilla movements in Argentina. As noted, Oesterheld was himself involved in one of these movements, and it cost him his life and that of his four daughters.

But that movement is not part of the Argentina of the late 1950s, nor is it part of Oesterheld's own artistic consciousness as he sets out to write the text for *El Eternauta*. Rather, the merits of *El Eternauta* lie with how Oesterheld is able to sustain his action narrative for almost four hundred pages; how he sets it up in terms of a narrative within a narrative; how, in the end, he seals it with a metanarrative contextualization that has the merit of raising the stakes for graphic action narratives: telling this story might just save the world. As the closing words state: "¿SERÁ POSIBLE?" ([Could it happen?] 366). If all of this is accomplished in the context of masculine privilege and the masculinist privilege of action graphic narratives, it is hardly surprising, given the work's overall contextualization in Argentine cultural production of sixty years ago and the unalloyed masculine dynamics of power in Argentina.[30]

CHAPTER 2

The Bar as Theatrical Heterotopia:
José Muñoz and Carlos Sampayo's *El Bar de Joe*

The space in which we live, which draws us out of ourselves, in which the erosion of our lives, our time and our history occurs, the space that claws and gnaws at us, is also, in itself, a heterogeneous space. In other words, we do not live in a kind of void, inside of which we could place individuals and things. We do not live inside a void that could be colored with diverse shades of light, we live inside a set of relations that delineates sites which are irreducible to one another and absolutely not superimposable on one another.

FOUCAULT, "OF OTHER SPACES, HETEROTOPIAS"

One can reasonably consider all heterotopic spaces as in some way privileged human arenas; perhaps, indeed, all such spaces are always sensed to be privileged in one way or another. We understand heterotopia in the Foucauldian sense as a lived human space that is supersaturated with meaning, one that is marked off, along any one or several sociosemantic axes, from the ordinary or everyday realms of human events, which do not immediately evince supersaturated meanings or relationships. Perhaps, in reality, all realms of human events are exponentially heterotopic. Heterotopic spaces, then—because they are marked as something other than the ground zero of humdrum existence that appears to have weak or tenuous interrelationships—become the preferred fields of cultural production: the brothel is more interesting than the bourgeois family room, the cult cabal is more engrossing than the mainline gospel service, the smoke-filled bar throbs with more fascinating human creatures than Saturday-night bingo. None of this may really be true, as great works of literature centering on the ground zero of the ordinary may attest. But our sociocultural imaginary is predicated on the assumption that there are marked and unmarked spaces of lived human experience, and that the latter may routinely be considered the most interesting ones.

Indeed, then, heterotopic spaces, as unique as they may be when viewed in conjunction with the so-called ordinary, can easily come to be perceived as microcosms of society as a whole, something like the ship-of-fools matrix, whereby perhaps the more heterotopic a space, the more synecdochical it is of human society, which is an ironic twist, since one could argue that the most ordinary of inhabited spaces ought to be the most representative of human society. Yet when it is a matter of social difference that drives cultural production, the marked heterotopic space emerges as the most intrinsically engaging one.

All societies seem to have an inventory of most frequently visited, so to speak, heterotopic spaces. Among these one of the most preferred is the bar, which can be drawn along the axes of out-of-the-way dive to sophisticated cocktail lounge, neighborhood tavern to refuge of the marginal (i.e., until recently, lesbian and gay bars), comfort zones (e.g., the English pub) to dives and dens of iniquity.

El Bar de Joe (originally published in French as *Le Bar à Joe* in 1981; Spanish translation published in Barcelona in 2005) by José Muñoz (illustrations; 1942–) and Carlos Sampayo (narrative text; 1943–) is one of the most popular texts of these Argentine artists, who abandoned their native Argentina in the 1970s and who have worked in Europe since then; *El Bar de Joe* is the first in a three-volume series that includes, to give their original titles in French, *Histoire amicable du Bar à Joe* (1987; Spanish translation as *Episodios amistosos* [2005]) and *Dans les bars* (2002; Spanish translation as *En los bares* [2005]), with the collective title of *Historias del bar*. Muñoz and Sampayo have produced several series, the gritty realism stories of which the eponymous Alack Sinner is the central character (eight titles published in French between 1977 and 2006, with some Spanish and English translations),[1] in addition to single books on musical artists such as Carlos Gardel (2007) and Billie Holiday (1991). Unquestionably, their work indicates much that is globalized about contemporary graphic fiction: their writing in a foreign language, their popularity in that language and in English translation, the fact that their work is available back in their native Argentina in translations published in Barcelona (which, thus, are characterized by the details of Peninsular rather than Argentine Spanish) and yet the fact that there is much in tone and texture in their work that is unmistakably Argentine (Sampayo studied with the legendary Alberto Breccia before leaving Argentina).

Indeed, *El Bar de Joe* is set in New York City[2] and has a noirish aspect to it where the urban spaces, the denizens of the night, the sordid criminal acts, and the unending stories of despair and degradation look as though they were inspired by Weegee's famous police photography (Arthur Fellig [1899–1968]). Weegee would somehow manage to make it to crime scenes before the police, and frequently one of the singular aspects of his photographs is the absence of the police, as though what were really happening was a series of violent quotidian events of life and not formally crimes, as defined by a police presence. The police are around in *El Bar de Joe*, although the commerce of human life, so much of which involves acts of violence, seems to take place as though they did not exist—i.e., we never see them engaging in "real" police work, only in creating an ambience of fear and harassment.[3]

Joe, who is both owner and chief bartender, presides over a bar that is nondescript in terms of its location and aspirational clientele. New York City is filled with such bars (as is Muñoz and Sampayo's native Buenos Aires, the only city in Latin America to have as unique a bar culture as New York City), and they may be found anywhere, as common a few doors down from an elegant hotel as in one of the many pockets of decay in mid-Manhattan or in one of the island's many fringe neighborhoods. The important detail about Joe's Bar, which also bears the name Joe's Music Bar, is that it functions as a variety show of liminal human nature. That is, while all heterotopic spaces can be cast as microcosms of the human spectacle, the bar belongs to a subcategory of heterotopic space in which there is an internal duplication of the gaze of the reader, a reader who is given extraordinary access to the space in question through the conventions of cultural production.

Since cultural production presupposes a reader (viewer, spectator, etc.), it does not necessarily engage in creating an internal duplication of this entity of the semiotic act. Yet one of the conventions of the bar as recurring referent of cultural production is that there are internal readers of that bar's comings and goings. In some cases, certain clients might fulfill that function: the nondescript guy at the end of the bar, overhearing everyone else's conversation, the lonely woman at a back table, nursing her drink as her eyes wander over the other customers. Or, paradigmatically, it is the barman, who looks out from the proscenium arch of the bar proper to the stage that is the area of the customers, with whom he might interact, but most of the time on whom he is keeping a steady eye, as much for commercial reasons as for reasons of security: their stories, which he overhears, listens to, contemplates, and sometimes intervenes in, are all triggers for potential violence that can cost him dearly, and not just if the police happen to show up or get called in.

J. Muñoz and C. Sampayo, *El Bar de Joe*

The opening full page, divided into three panels, is indicative of the world of Joe's bar and his concerns. Joe, who bears a striking resemblance to the Mexican composer and singer Agustín Lara, a man who spent his own share of time in notorious Mexican watering holes, can be seen at the top of the second panel, slightly to the right of center, where he is telling one of the other barmen that his stomach hurts, no doubt from the ulcer-producing tensions of his job. If Joe is not present in the other two panels, it is because he is viewing the proceedings in the room from the same perspective as we the readers are. This is especially evident in the way in which the musicians are across the room from in front of him—that is, from his proscenium arch position behind the bar—and in the third panel, the musicians are situated directly across the room from the reader's vantage point, which, then, would be where Joe is standing. The precise perspective vis-à-vis Joe is not indicated in the first panel, but all three panels are correlative in that they represent different views of the customer space—the theatrical arena, if you will—of Joe's bar.

There is no need to enumerate in detail the approximately three dozen inhabitants of this space (perhaps more because it is not always evident how many individuals are included in a particular group, especially since the dialogue boxes obscure many in the background). Clearly this is the sort of mix of clientele one might expect to find in New York City, a veritable Noah's ark of the demographic spectrum of the city. All we receive are snippets of their conversation. Some conversations are apparently standard New York intellectual chic, such as the exchange between the presumed Arabic sheik and the young woman to the left of the third panel; others are elliptical, suggestive of barely contained violence either in the tenor of their enunciation or the human drama behind them. And others, such as the comments of the shoeshine boy decked out in war medals, who occupies the center of the first panel, and is almost lost over the shoulder of the female partner in the intellectual conversation in the third panel, come off as delivered in flat monotones that indicate an automated enunciation that is the product of years of saying the same thing because there is nothing else to say—as much as one might be struck by the circumstances of a decorated soldier turned shoeshine boy, a black man who served as a sergeant and never anything more than that in three successive US wars. A circumstance that unquestionably speaks volumes regarding the social history of minorities in America, one of the many deplorable facets of the social history of the country to be found ensconced in bars like Joe's, as though it were the end of the line.

In fact, it is for the aging shoeshine boy, Jonathan Jones, who must easily be eighty years old or more, that *El Bar de Joe* is divided into five discretely titled stories. As is often the case in stories brought together in a single volume of graphic narrative (as is the case of the Galera-Coutinho and Moon-Bá volumes discussed elsewhere in this study), there are elements of interrelatedness between them, not just the locale (in this case, the bar) but in narrative threads, and characters in them, that show up from one story to the other.

The opening triptych I have just been discussing is the first page of the story "Pepe el arquitecto" [Pepe the Architect]. Although executed long before the anti-immigrant hysteria of the past decade or so in the United States, this story centers on the increasing paranoia of Pepe, an illegal immigrant who trained as an architect in his native Mexico. While we are not told how he ends up in New York City, he has no work papers, and, as he states, he can't get them without a steady job, and he can't get a steady job without papers (15). Pepe does have a job of sorts, which involves cleaning up the bar at the end of the night, along with Joe and Jonathan, which allows him to pay for modest living quarters nearby. Constantly fearful that he will be picked up by the police, jailed, beaten, deported, one night he is assaulted by a woman, whom he at first takes for the police. Crazy or simply sex-crazed, she forces him to take her back to his place, where she attacks him in more ways than just sexually. She tears up the memento picture he has of himself with his parents and then attempts to destroy his passport, after breaking his glasses, in what appears to be a pattern of psychological domination that goes beyond the transitorily sexual. He eventually knocks her out and flees with his passport, convinced that the police will, more than ever, be on his trail.

When he shows up at Joe's, Joe, who has treated him with some humanity, plies him with drink, although he quickly passes out. When he comes to, Joe offers him a place to stay—living in the bar with Jonathan. Pepe goes berserk, unable to respond appropriately to Joe's offer (he says no one has ever offered him anything [31]) and attacks Jonathan, in a paradigmatic example of the syndrome of one underdog against another, as a pitiful and supine victim of the miseries of the American dream, an accomplice of the system. This is the sort of contestational discourse Jonathan is not equipped to comprehend, and he threatens to turn Pepe in. Pepe flees into the night, and he is discovered dead by a passerby, one of Joe's patrons, who calls the police but won't identify himself. Propped up against a trash can, Pepe is one more piece of garbage in the dystopian city. One might insist that the world outside the bar enlarges the heterotopia of the bar: New York City, or cities like it that harbor many such spaces as Joe's bar, are heterotopias in a context that might possibly subscribe to the utopian belief that there is an urban setting that is the realm of ordinary, decent, respectable life to which New York City is the grim dystopian exception. But of course, for the social realities being presented here, this is not true, and Joe's bar as depicted here would tend to validate the assertion that presumed heterotopic spaces are not marked exceptions to a homogeneous normality, but marked exemplars of the world at large. They only appear to be abnormal in nature.

The one time in the five stories in which we see Joe as anything other than an ulcer-plagued observer of his own corner of the dystopia is after he has left Pepe and Jonathan to argue over Pepe's fate. As he walks through the predawn streets, only to be challenged by the police but not detained because he is a white American with his papers in order (!), Joe meditates, in a fashion befitting a reflective spectator, on the nature of his clients, Pepe in particular. Joe knows he must support his clients in the same way that the audience is called on to support the actors, each one in his own theatrical sphere. Joe's form of applause is being agreeable to and with his clients: "Me paso la vida diciéndole que sí a todo el mundo" ([I spend my whole life saying yes to everybody] 32), although he is disconcerted when Pepe apparently breaks the rules or violates the conventions. Pepe will, as we have seen, disappear from the scene, but there will always be other "tíos" ([guys] this word is a touch of Peninsular Spanish in the language of the narrative) to take his place, and Joe, the audience of one in the realm that is his bar, will not want for additional, if, in the end, not very variegated, human dramas to witness.

The other four stories consist of a hired assassin who befriends his victim in "Wilcox & Conrad"; "Historias oxidadas" [Rusty stories], about a has-been boxer; "Ella" [She], who is an urban photographer of the sort the city abounds in; and "Quinta historia" [Fifth story], a gritty tale of young love in the style of the American graphic artist Robert Crumb's tales of the city. (Indeed, if Crumb's work seems to exude the rancid sweat and urine of cheap urban housing, Muñoz and Sampayo's depiction of Joe's bar, particularly as a setting for young love, nauseates one thinking of the stale smoke and alcoholic vapors the place is rife with).

"Ella" stands out among these stories because it, too, is built on internal duplication, although in this case the spectator from within is a supplement to Joe, a photographer who hangs out at his bar, assembling

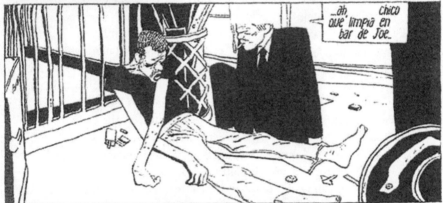

J. Muñoz and C. Sampayo, *El Bar de Joe*

a photographic dossier of its habitués. In fact, the first panel of the story shows her apartment with its dark room and, on the wall, one of her images, which the text labels Joe's Old Bar, called simply Joe's: clearly the addition of musicians in his new space enables him to transition to the more upscale name, Joe's Music Bar. The photographer, a youngish woman who remains nameless, blends in with the rest of the clients, except for the presence of her camera, which she does not, like other urban photographers concerned over the possible hostility of their subjects, attempt to hide. As for the archive of images she has assembled, she dedicates herself to blowing them up, although the text does not specify a reason such as making them more lifelike or attempting to discover some secret, in the fashion of Julio Cortázar's "Las babas del diablo" [Devil's slobber], they may have hidden in them.[4]

That the photographer is a woman is particularly significant. Bars are paradigmatic male spaces.[5] With the exception of lesbian bars, which may insist, for reasons of sexism and homophobia, on a no-men-admitted policy, bars are dominated by male owners, male barmen, and male patrons.[6] Although today women are freer to enter bars like Joe's on their own without being taken necessarily for prostitutes,[7] at the time the narrative was written, single women in bars might have been more suspect.[8] The phenomenon of lonely women seeking companionship in bars is an old one, thematicized in much cultural production, especially in nighttime or early-morning-hours settings. The woman who attacks Pepe in the first story of *El Bar de Joe* sees him on her forays to the bar, although when she does come on to him, she chooses to corner him, police style, in an alley outside the bar (he at first thinks she is a police officer).

Although photographers are paradigmatically loners, especially those who wander the streets looking for photographic subjects (e.g., Garry Winogrand, whose spontaneous street photography in New York is legendary) and as opposed to someone like the aforementioned Weegee, who went to shoot images in response to emergency police calls, there is a generalized pathos attached to a woman as a photographer loner.[9] Muñoz and Sampayo very much pick up on this dimension of the virtually anonymous Ella, who spies, so to speak, with her camera on the human interactions of her fellow bar patrons. In this way, the photographer is also a privileged spectator, and her images become an archive of the heterotopic space that is the bar. For her they are a formal registry of whatever it is she is seeking in her life in the bar.

But not all of "Ella" is focused on the bar. The woman has a recurring obsession that she is ill with cancer, although she confesses that the analyses she has had done came back negative. In moments of panic over her suspected illness, she rushes to an emergency room, where she meets a tender and considerate African American doctor (still rare in the United States in the early 1980s). He becomes for her a real human being, not just the object of her camera's one-eyed impersonal gaze, and the focus of interest of her two-eyed direct personal gaze (87). Seeing in him a soul mate, she can nevertheless only approach him obliquely through her camera: "Fotografías de un año y medio de historia personal. Fotografías en la que Ella no aparece ni una sola vez, como si le bastase la fugacidad del espejo: restituye su imagen, pero también la disimula al no reflejarla" (87).[10] This text is accompanied by images of Ella roaming the city with her camera, attempting to find the doctor, although in the process amassing images of people with whom she has no personal involvement. These photographs constitute a personal history both in the sense of their being the record of her quest and in that she is absent from them, not just because she is on the other side of the camera, but because they do not in any way involve her emotionally, which is how I take the reference to the nonreflecting mirror of the quote above. When she does on one occasion encounter the doctor, she lowers her camera and approaches him directly.

An on-and-off relationship, which becomes fully sexual, develops between the two of them, although Ella continues to frequent the streets with her camera, even abandoning their lover's bed early one morning to return to the streets: "Quiero aprovechar la luz del amanecer para hacer fotos. Quiero estar sola para pensar en ti y recordarte" (90).[11] This is not a strange statement coming from a committed professional photographer; what is strange is that she does not take images of their relationship, either as casual photographs or as a record of their lovemaking.[12]

When the doctor does not keep a date with her and subsequently disappears, Ella sinks into despair. At one point, her own life now supposedly interesting (she has tears streaming down her face), she becomes the object of the gaze of other street photographers (94), and she photographs them photographing her in a mise en abyme effect in which the photographer becomes the photographed in the way in which the presumed use of photography here, the Sontagian record of the pain of others, disappears in the suggested receding reflections of juxtaposed lenses. But her pain is not recorded by her, and its capture by the other photographers is only evident in her image of their camera directed toward her as a subject worthy of their recording. As one photographer says to her companion, "¡Ésa, ésa! Mira, está llorando" (94; [That woman, that one! Look, she's crying!]).

J. Muñoz and C. Sampayo, *El Bar de Joe*

    Ella continues her photography in Joe's bar (there is another incident of narrative intersection with one of the other stories) until the doctor appears one night, saying he knew he would find her in the bar (97). She attempts to revive their relationship, but he is evasive, changed, although some physical intimacy occurs between them and he attempts to put a ring on her finger at the same time he repeatedly tells her goodbye. She tosses the ring in the garbage, saying it has nothing to do with them (100). Her despair returns, but after days of isolation, she returns to the street with her camera: "Sale en busca de algo" [She goes out in search of something]. This phrase becomes ironic, since it could mean "in search of whatever might happen along" or "in search of something specific." The first interpretation makes sense as she takes some random images, but the second meaning affirms itself when she spots the doctor and a male friend, consulting a magazine together, unaware of her presence; for the first time, the doctor is dressed in a casual—ethnic?—fashion. As she raises her camera to photograph them, the panel transitions to a smaller one in which the two men walk off hand in hand. The final page has her returning home, pinning the last photographic image to

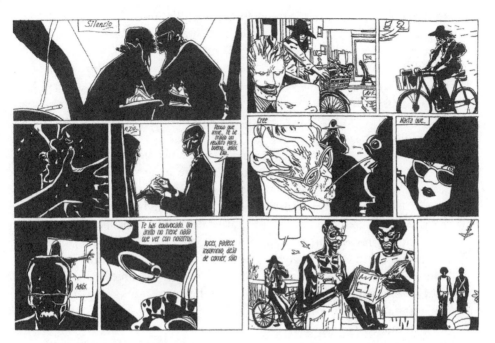

J. Muñoz and C. Sampayo, *El Bar de Joe*

the wall (that of the doctor and his male lover? The one of the boxer she has photographed in the bar who has, according to the newspaper she buys, just committed suicide?), picking up an international plane ticket she has purchased and walking out the door, clicking the lights off.

This final gesture and the ambiguity as to which final photograph she has put up on her wall speak to the futility of her work, to the vanishing point, one might say, of her photographic project. Murder (although she doesn't know the man she photographs at one point in the bar is a hired hit man), suicide, apparently permanent loss (her casting the doctor's ring in the trash can foreshadows her realization that, even if she wanted to, there can be no lasting relationship with the man who gave it to her) are here all indexes of the destruction of life. Her photography is an attempt to register life and, apparently as she preserves the images and amplifies them as though looking for a secret meaning, to give it a sense of unity and coherence. We don't know if her flight will be permanent,[13] but the final gesture of turning out the lights consigns her photographic work to darkness and oblivion, as though through some technical mistake the images never existed. Perhaps this is all a gesture toward the necessary healing and forgetting Ella must face up to, al-though her mental health, as seen in her paranoia over being ill with cancer, does not seem too promising. Perhaps it is her suicidal renunci-ation of life as it is exemplified in the theatrical heterotopia of Joe's Bar that she turned herself into a privileged witness—indeed, privileged ar-chivist—of. Perhaps it is the implicit rejection of art—the graphic novel-ist's, the street photographer's—and any possibility of making sense of the world.

Muñoz and Sampayo, by creating a noirish ambience with Joe's bar, underscore the way in which heterotopic space is, in the last analysis, a figure of human society: such space is more interestingly representa-tive of lived human experience than presumedly nonheterotopic, ordi-nary, everyday spaces. Image and narrative text often work against each other in the instance of ambiguity I have noted, and this is reasonable, since no one can ever know quite what it is that's going on in the world, why anything takes place at all, or why individual social subjects do what they seem compelled to do.[14] Willcox, the hit man, thanks Conrad for his hospitality after they become good friends in Joe's bar by giving him a set of rare stamps (they are both consummate collectors) right before he kills him. Willcox is at a loss to explain his actions and sees the matter of the stamps as an alarm signal. But an alarm signal of what? He is left to muse "Debería jubilarme? . . ." ([Maybe I should retire] 58), which is what Ella, in a sense, has chosen to do at the end of her story. It is all, as Joe himself recognizes in my discussion of his relationship with Pepe, in the end nothing more than a question of "ese bar de mierda" ([this shitty bar] 32).

CHAPTER 3

Resisting Tyranny: The *Perramus* Figure of Alberto Breccia and Juan Sasturain

The main impetus for Perramus was the need to testify to everything that happened in Argentina during the era of military dictatorship. Drawings were and still are my only weapon.
ROMMENS 315

Alberto Breccia (1919–1993) is one of the most legendary names in Argentine graphic narrative, known as much for his work in conventional comic strips and for his edgy contributions to what we are here calling graphic narrative. Indeed, his narrative works like *Ernie Pike* in the 1950s and *Mort Cinder* in the 1960s, to name only two of the most prominent, are really graphic narratives *avant-la-lettre* and not really comic books in the general sense of popular art and facile reading codes. These are stories with discursive and verbal density, and the art is hardly of the simplistic-line-drawings variety. The innovative and experimental nature of Breccia's work is perhaps most revealed in his undertaking, in 1969, to reimagine the graphic representation of *El Eternauta*, the most venerable of Argentine graphic narratives, moving the artwork of the science-fiction text away from the quite transparent style of the original artist, Francisco Solana López, and toward a menacing chiaroscuro that complicated Oesterheld's fairly straightforward narrative of masculine heroics in times of social crisis (see the chapter in this study on Oesterheld's narrative).

Breccia's experiment with menacing chiaroscuro is very much in evidence in the four stories that make up the three volumes of the *Perramus* series: *El piloto del olvido* [The raincoat of oblivion][1] and *El alma de la ciudad* [The soul of the city] (originally published in French in 1986 and in Spanish in Argentina in 1987); *La isla del guano* [Guano island] (published separately as *Perramus 3* in both French and Spanish); and *Diente por diente* [Tooth for a tooth] (published separately as *Perramus 4* in French in 1991 and in Spanish in 2006). There are numerous translations into German, as well as single works translated into Danish and Italian. Each of the *Perramus* stories—I repeat, four total, in three volumes, with a recent publication of the four in a single volume—is divided into about a dozen chapters, the consequence of how this material was published, outside Argentina, throughout the early 1980s while the military dictatorship was still in effect.[2]

Perramus is one of those graphic novels, like the Fábio Moon–Gabriel Bá or Daniel Galera texts studied elsewhere in this monograph, where the reader is immediately struck by the complex originality of the graphic image; this is reinforced by the abundance of panels (say, unlike *El Eternauta,* where the sometimes mundane, sometimes catchy drawings are overwhelmed by the dominance of the verbal text) where no verbal text appears and the reader's gaze roams over panels of varying sizes in which a highly expressionistic representation challenges anyone's desire for immediate signifying transparency. This is obvious from the cover of the first Spanish edition (1987; first published in Barcelona, and in its parallel Argentine edition sponsored in part by the government's program of Ediciones Culturales Argentinas).

Breaking with one tradition of graphic narrative in which the geographic locale is eminently evident (as in *El Eternauta*), Breccia's freeze-frames of the Latin American, Argentine, Buenos Aires landscape are essentially unrecognizable: no belle époque buildings, no Avenida Nueve de Julio anchored by the Obelisco, no paradigmatic Porteño café, no elegant tree-lined residential barrio. The cityscape is barren; trees are leafless; buildings bulk in massive irregular shapes that come off as menacing monoliths, anthropomorphized monsters ready to leap out at the lone pedestrian; sidewalks are narrow channels whose surfaces look like sewer waters about to carry the pedestrians away to subterranean cisterns; the sky, which is frequently cloudy in humidity-bound Buenos Aires, seems more composed of chunks of cement than puffy masses. One of the truly distinctive aspects of Breccia's drawings, particularly effective in his decision to work in gray tones because of the possibilities of transitional blurring of outlines, borders, and points of contact between objects, is that they appear to have been inspired by what one sees through a powerful biomedical microscope: surface textures appear to be the inside of microbic cells, strings or chains of molecules, smears of globulin-like substances. The way in which different textures overlap across the boundaries of what one would ordinarily perceive as distinct and differentiated objects gives the effect of expanding disease-bearing substances, effectively consonant with the pervasive infection of everyday life by the military tyranny.

The agents of the latter here are not identified metonymically as the "generals," as they were commonly designated during the twentieth-century military regimes in Argentina (particularly the neofascist one that held power between 1976–1983 and upon whose demise there occurs the outburst of revisionist cultural production of which *Perramus* is an early example).[3] The metonym of this top rank of the army was meant to include that of the other armed forces that constituted the absolutist authoritarian ruling Juntas, and, as a sign for the prevalence of military rank, it signaled the entire apparatus of repression, in the form of an extensive application of unquestionable and rigid discipline, that sought to dominate the citizenry in the name of (as the Brazilian flag says) order and progress. Rather, the texts by Juan Sasturain (1945–) refer to the *mariscales*, the marshals, in one sense the supra-ranked military authority that comes out of the Roman tradition of the individual charged with maintaining discipline and imposing punishment for violations of it. To this extent, the text underscores the most draconian level of tyrannical power. Therefore, Breccia's graphic representation of the military is almost exclusively in terms of such an exalted rank, marked by the omnipresence of the *pocho*, the high-peaked formal uniform hat made popular by Juan Domingo Perón and ever after associated with the mythification of military preeminence in the authoritarian state (whether democratically elected, as in the case of Perón [1946–1955, 1973–1974], or de facto, as in the case of the three dictatorships that followed his ouster [1955–1958, 1966–1973, 1976–1983]). Concomitantly, the marshals are uniformly represented as frightening skulls as a metaphor of the pall of mortal corruption they cast across the nightmarish, apocalyptical cityscape Breccia depicts.

As a text written subsequent to the long period of military tyranny, particularly the neofascist dictatorship of 1976–1983, a period often characterized as "los años de plomo" (the leaden years, whose leaden texture Breccia depicts in such effective artistic terms), it allowed for a meditation, via cultural production, on the substance of daily life during the regime. Sasturain's two stories in the original *Perramus* collection very much capture the uprooted solitude of the individual in the person of the main character, a man who loses his memory and begins to rebuild it by first taking as his name the label of an abandoned item of masculine outerwear, Perramus, the name of a venerable Argentine high-end clothier dating back to the early twentieth century and the years of greatest prosperity and socioeconomic growth in Argentina. Perramus, as the cover makes clear, is Raymond Chandler's lone man of principle traversing the mean streets of the city.[4] Thus, it is reasonable for the reader of *Perramus* to be drawn to the ways in which the visible military presence is made manifest; the psychological or emotional effects are present—in a necessarily indirect manifestation (since they are first internal and then perhaps externally projected)—in the behavior of individuals, which I will deal with when specifically characterizing Sasturain's storylines. Although numerically in the minority, the agents of military repression crowd, clog, disrupt the spontaneous movement of the citizenry in these strips. In their often sudden massed appearance, they overwhelm citizens, subduing them with the unabashed use of extreme forms of violence. In their application of unchecked violence and in their unrestrained movement from one point to another, they destroy anything along their path of movement. Thus, along with the destructive flow of their movement, the indiscriminate blasts of bullets and mortars leave in their wake the apocalyptic cityscape Breccia's characterization of the city privileges.

In one panel, the writer Jorge Luis Borges, whose presence in *Perramus* is crucial and really rather stunning (more on that later),[5] speaks of supporting at one time the Conservative Party in the mistaken belief that they could preserve something meaningful of the past.[6] This ideologeme of the conservatives is a grounding principle of the military dictatorship that they support, the idea that there is an "eternal" Argentine essence that must be protected and perpetuated. Yet the military's transit across the traditional urban landscape, the visible manifestation of the multiple heritages of the city, is only and always one of mayhem and destruction. In this fashion, Breccia projects Borges's words outside his apartment so that the reader understands them in the context of the apocalyptic, post-holocaust texture of the city: as Borges speaks, we see an empty city, the outlines of its buildings and spaces of human activities (places of business, cafés, bookstores, and the like) represented more like jumbled pieces of a jigsaw puzzle than a coherent realm of human activity. The street is dominated by the hulking presence of heavily armed soldiers, and the constructed environment is more one of cavernous ruins than of well-articulated architectural undertakings.

This is the landscape through which Perramus moves. He is the survivor of one of the murderous operations of *grupos de tarea*, the

A. Breccia and L. Sasturain, *Perramus*

blitzkrieg-like storm troopers, agents in civilian clothes accompanied by police units, whose bureaucratic designation, "working groups," masked the violence of their tactics. As they descend upon Perramus (who, of course, does not yet have this name) and his sleeping comrades, he abandons them and flees over the rooftops of the city to safety. Racked by guilt, he ends up in the arms of a prostitute (Sasturain has a soft spot for the sentimental figure of the prostitute with the heart of gold), who lends him the raincoat left behind (we are in one of the legendary waterfront brothels of a Buenos Aires red-light district long, long gone) by a Swedish sailor. Since the man's memory has been cleansed of his past in the act of consoling sex, it is that coat's label that gives Perramus his new name and the point of departure for building a new identity. It will be that of the moral man who, single-handedly and then with some sidekicks, will attempt to do good in the world.[7] Specifically, this eponymic hero of the initial story, *El piloto del olvido* [The raincoat of oblivion], will undertake a series of operations that defy and resist military tyranny.[8] Specifically, Perramus will become involved in a question of espionage that involves the resistance to the military regime and, in the first approximation to the controversial figure of Borges, Sasturain's story will involve a sonnet by the Baroque Spanish poet Francisco de Quevedo, read by Borges in a public lecture, the detention of a member of the audience who asked Borges a question about the sonnet (the insinuation is that she is part of a guerrilla movement for which the sonnet is the cipher to a key piece of information), the madam from the waterfront brothel who deciphers the meaning hidden in the sonnet, and the prostitute who provided him emotional succor and the raincoat and, now, the confirmation of his existential redemption and the entrée into the space of a new moral adventure.

Frankly, one is a bit disappointed by the quality of Sasturain's narrative, the work of a competent but undistinguished author whose storyline is a bit diffuse and not always tightly integrated into a strongly articulated meaning. This is, for example, the case with the sequence relating to a stereotypical villain, Mr. Whitesnow Island Co., of US support for and collaboration with the Latin American military regimes (chapters 3–4 of *El piloto*), and with a phony director of American Westerns, Sam [Peckinpah?], who only films and sells previews of feature-length films he never makes (chapters 5–6). This is supposedly a riff on American cultural exploitation of Latin America.

Where *El piloto* and *El alma de la ciudad,* the second narrative published in the first *Perramus* edition, become truly interesting is with the appearance as a character of the now world-renowned Argentine writer Jorge Luis Borges (1899–1986). Oswaldo Soriano, in his introduction to the *Perramus* set of stories, characterizes the importance of Borges's emergence here and the way in which the Sasturain–Breccia collaboration constitutes a homage to the writer who had recently died in Geneva. Borges provoked controversy, and it often seemed that he reveled in being vilified more than he tolerated adulation: it is widely believed he went to Geneva to die precisely in order to avoid being the object of a media-circus state funeral as the country's greatest writer. It is also customarily believed in Argentina that one must be recognized in Paris— i.e., anywhere important abroad—before it can be possible to receive acceptance in the unforgiving milieu of cultural prestige in Buenos Aires. Of course, as is well known, Borges's problems did not come from the bourgeois literary circles, with all their demanding rituals and institutions, but from the left, the revolutionary left of the 1950s–1980s, for whom Adolfo Prieto's damning concluding characterization (in the first book-length study of Borges, published in 1954) that Borges represented the "inutilidad de cierta literatura" ([The uselessness of some literature] 90), someone one could do without or do well to ignore and forget, was absolutely determinate.

The fact that Borges was the darling of foreign literary establishments showed how un-Argentine he was. His politics were (as mentioned above) scandalously aligned with the right; he had an uncomfortable relationship with Spanish (especially with what he saw as the overblown pretensions of an Argentine intellectual and artistic elite) as well as a complicated—often negative—relationship with Argentine popular culture, such as the so-called national epic, the *Martín Fierro* (1872 and 1876), and the tango. To be sure, Borges's positions often moved around, as part of the intensity of his consideration of the dimensions of cultural production and the take-no-prisoners nature of his relish for controversy. It is almost quaint now to read the characterization of Prieto and his followers (Foster, "Adolfo Prieto") as serious, rather than *parti-pris*, critical consideration of his writing able to grasp and demonstrate how his intellectual and artistic commitments were of a whole with the preponderance of values associated with human rights and the resistance to repression and tyranny, whether right or left. Soriano, in his explicit comments on the presence of Borges in the Sasturain–Breccia collaboration (I place the writer's name first here, since his storyline is the point of origin for the text), does not characterize what the bases or the timeframe for Borges's embrace by a major-

ity of Argentine cultural institutions were. But by implication in the stories themselves, one senses the emergence of an appreciation for the way
in which Borges transmitted a sense of the dignity of human experience
that was threatened by the military regime, despite all of its high-volume
rhetoric about the eternal Argentine character, the salvation of Western
civilization, the privilege accorded to conservative Christian principles,
and the mystic primacy of praetorian order over crass civil chaos.

Not that Borges is mystified by Sasturain and Breccia. Although he
is accorded more dignity of presence than he usually got from the left
or populist persuasions (one recalls here the way in which the masterful
cartoonist Roberto Fontanarrosa mocked Borges in his Inodoro Pereyra
strips [see Foster, "Fontanarrosa's *Gauchomania* and *Gauchophobia,*"
50–51]), there is something fustian about the way in which he sets up
the undertaking for capturing the "soul of the city" in the second narrative of the original *Perramus* collection, an undertaking that is based on
a revision of his famous story "La muerte y la brújula" ([Death and the
compass] 1942), in which a clever detective "solves" the pattern of a series of killings, only to discover that he has fallen victim to a labyrinthine
scheme to entrap him as the final victim. Although Borges's new labyrinth is intellectually ingenious, it leads to the dirty and mean streets of
the city and to the grossness of human conduct that could have had no
place in Borges's own fictional imaginary.

Nevertheless, *El alma de la ciudad* is an intriguing idea, and the
proposition of discovering, in all of the morass of corruption and degradation that are the apocalyptic consequences of military tyranny, a central core of the soul of the city, is a clear response to the moral clichés of
the ideology of repression. What is found is not so much a transcendent
soul that would satisfy moralistic pretentions, whether those of the military, of the guerrilla resistance, or of a post-1983 redemocratized Argentina. Rather, what is discovered is a panoply of human phenomena that
is presumably something more like the blood-and-guts substance of the
national identity than the bad-faith abstractions, written in capital letters, of the military's Proceso de Reorganización Nacional, which is how
the neofascist dictatorship inaugurated by Jorge Rafael Videla in 1976
characterized itself.

The opening panel of *El alma de la ciudad* firmly anchors the story in
the Buenos Aires of Jorge Luis Borges,[9] and the lower-left-hand corner
bears his affirmation that "La ciudad es como un plano de mis humillaciones y fracasos . . ." [The city is like a map of my humiliations and fail-
ures].[10] We do not know who makes the tandem comment "¿Qué hace-
mos ahora en la ciudad de los mariscales?" [What are we to do now in

the city of the marshals?], although the insinuation of the following panels, which focus individually on Perramus and his two sidekicks, is that it is Perramus himself who utters it. The balloon containing the question floats over what has become by now the signature image of the city under military tyranny: the gloomy mass of urban architecture that overwhelms the pedestrian, the shadowy (it seems at times almost imperceptible) presence of armed uniform patrols, and the omnipresent twisted and denuded tree that is almost an iconic presence throughout the representations of the landscape, something like a dying tree of life, the only evident trace of vegetation (and this in a city that has close to seven hundred parks, plazas, and squares) in a world in the advanced stages of decay and collapse. The close, cramped, stifling space of Breccia's images of the city contrasts dramatically with the documentary evidence of, despite being the third largest city in Latin America, how Buenos Aires is really a city of broad vistas and abundant open spaces, with (in contrast to São Paulo, the second largest city in Latin America) very little in the way of dense islands of mega-skyscrapers. Yet Breccia's expressionistic representation of the city speaks directly to the sense of being psychologically or emotionally overwhelmed by the omnipresent military domination.

Perramus's question is, one must note, semantically ambiguous in a crucial way, since it will constitute the point of departure for the second story about to be told. On the one hand, the question has the sense of "How did we end up in the city of the marshals?" as though there were some hidden forces that put into motion a chain of events that led them to that unpropitious destination. In fact, the conclusion of the previous story will play with the semantic ambiguity of the Spanish word *destino*, in the sense of "destination" (i.e., the city of the marshals) and "Destiny" (Perramus as a man of moral character destined to resist tyranny on behalf of others). *Destino* is a key word in the Quevedo sonnet that figures prominently in *El piloto del olvido*, and, as Borges observes, *destino* and *sentido* (meaning) are anagrams of each other: Perramus's destination/destiny is now the (re)acquired meaning of his life.

The second sense of Perramus's opening interrogative in *El alma de la ciudad* is "What are we going to do [now] in this city of the marshals?" The first sense implies that perhaps it would be best to get out, and this is what Perramus explicitly says in the second panel.

However, the three men find themselves with Borges in his study, and the poet proceeds to engage them in his cultural preoccupations. They go on to play a game of *truco* (literally, "deceit"), an Argentine equivalent of poker. But the lights go out and they comment on how

A. Breccia and L. Sasturain, *Perramus*

the city seems to disappear (Sasturain identifies the city as Santa María, the name the Uruguayan Juan Carlos Onetti uses in his novels set in a riverside city like Buenos Aires, whose original name was Santa María del Buen Aire [Ayre]). This is the only case in which Breccia's representation of the city lightens the gray shade so that there is now a preponderance of white. But it is not the white of the so-called City of Light (Paris, with which Porteños are often wont, in hyperbolic fashion, to compare Buenos Aires). Rather it is the white of what fades away, the loss of shading; the loss of material existence. The city still remains twisted, unbalanced, predominantly an incongruous mass of cement. As Borges observes—Borges, the supposed apolitical writer, blind literally and figuratively to the material presence of Buenos Aires—it is not only the citizenry that disappears, but the very city itself. As he further observes, the battle is not for the material presence of the city, but what is in the balance is the very soul of the city. At this point the principal narrative thrust of *El alma de la ciudad* comes into play.

Sasturain engages in a rather interesting revision of one of Borges's signature stories, mentioned above, "La muerte y la brújula." But this time the story is not of interest for its development of a plot of revenge against a detective who is far too rational for his own good, as he becomes enmeshed in a plot partially of his own making that will turn him into the last in a series of victims predicted by a geometric overlay of the city. In Sasturain's story, a double overlay is created (based on the Star of David, which subtly harks back to the Jewish elements in "La muerte").[11] Whereas Borges's original story had four points of reference (or, in the ad hoc labyrinth designed to ensnare the detective, three points meant to correlate with that of the first point, that of the circumstantial murder), the Star of David provides six points, six geographic locales of the city (Liniers; Devoto; Palermo; Retiro; Constitución; Nueva Pompeya; and the little-known central point, Plaza Escondida). In turn, as emerges through the succeeding chapters—one each devoted to the six points—these points correspond, after the inclusion of a seventh point (the center of the intersecting lines of the star), to seven days of the week, the seven notes of the C-major scale, seven individuals (actually, six human beings and a cat) whose first names (single name, in the case of the cat) are the names in Spanish of the notes of the musical scale (e.g., do, re, mi). Finally, the stories of each individual associated with one of the seven cardinal points (who are not victims, in the sense of the original Borges story, but icons of the life of the city) exemplify in turn each one of the seven deadly sins.

A. Breccia and L. Sasturain, *Perramus*

One might expect, given the moral commitment to the salvation of victims of the repression that motivates Perramus, the protagonists of each of the seven stories to incarnate one of the seven saintly virtues. But this is real life, not eschatological allegory, and this is Buenos Aires, a city of man[12] and hardly a city of God, despite its ironically saintly name. Indeed, several of the segments are driven by rather grossly outrageous narrative propositions, such as the one corresponding to Villa Devoto/Thursday/Falo (the note fa), which requires an imprisoned rapist (his nickname means "phallus" in Spanish) to come to orgasm with a series of grotesque prostitutes in order to determine the release of fellow prisoners (he fails, but his attempts are graphically detailed).

In the end, when the pattern has become clear to Perramus and his sidekicks and when the former has walked away in disgust at what he believes to be merely one of Borges's much-vaunted intellectual games, there is, nevertheless, the sense that an accurate portrayal of the creatural materiality of the city has been afforded. This might not be a catalog of the themes of Borges's *ficciones*, but it serves to basically characterize Argentine cultural production.

Yet Perramus might well ask, as he does, whether the city has been saved after all. One of Perramus's sidekicks seems to think that Borges and Perramus are two sides of the same coin, presumably in the Borgean sense of the compulsion to explain what cannot be explained in human existence; nevertheless, despite vowing to create their own adventures, they end up rejoining Borges and Perramus. Perhaps this is rather a lame ending if the main thrust of the narrative is identification and salvaging of the soul of the city. But perhaps, then, it is consonant with the way in which what becomes revealed in the pursuit of the geometric framework Borges has set up constitutes not a gallery of national heroes who embody paradigmatically the transcendent human virtues. Rather, the seven embodiments of Everyman are no better or worse than anybody else. I suppose where this makes sense in the sociohistorical context of *Perramus* is the recovery of the plain ordinariness of human existence, quite at odds with the highly spiritualized slogans of the dictatorship and its self-attributed mission to save Argentina from itself as a bulwark or bastion of Christianity and Western Civilization, a project that was to be conducted by engaging in a program of state terrorism against the citizenry. One way of viewing *Perramus* is as a depiction of the tremendous ironies of such an ideological formulation: the citizenry is no better or worse than one might expect, the essence of human nature as summarized by the seven deadly sins, and the Saviors of the Fatherland are merely as they showed themselves to be, neofascist assassins.

CHAPTER 4

The Lion in Winter: Carlos Sampayo and Francisco Solano López's Police Commissioner Evaristo

Y para eso estaba yo como un esclavo de la Ley [. . .]
[That's why I was there as a slave to the Law]
MENESES 195

In organizing a commentary on police commissioner Evaristo, it is inevitable that one re-evoke Raymond Chandler's previously cited lone man of principle traversing the mean streets of the city.[1] It is of only relative consequence that Sampayo and Solano López's Evaristo is a police commissioner rather than the freelance gumshoe we find in Chandler's novels. In the latter case, Philip Marlowe must, in fact, struggle against the pervasive corruption of the highest police hierarchy of Bay City (a thinly disguised Santa Monica, California), while in the Argentines' *Evaristo* (1985),[2] Evaristo's realm is the Municipality of Buenos Aires police, where he is ranged against both incompetency and corruption in his own ranks and the corruption of those who see the police force as a personal service agency. It is significant that while the narratives echo the American ideologeme of the solitary warrior ranged against the forces of evil (which is, after all, the one most abiding theme in the classic and highly influential American comic-book narratives), Evaristo[3] is hardly idealized in the tradition of Dick Tracy (Tracy is a part of the system), Batman (Batman is a supplement to the system, in the sense that he collaborates with Gotham City's police chief), or Superman (Superman operates entirely outside of the establishment).

Evaristo is a former heavyweight prizefighter who has thickened considerably over the years, although he is still solidly muscular, and he is not afraid to use his pugilistic prowess, backed up by his appreciable heft, to impart punches when he is pushed to the limit or even, in

C. Sampayo and F. Solano López, *Evaristo*

one case, to kick a beat officer senseless for having himself used violence against a street urchin. In these cases, Evaristo falls back on the considerable impunity of the police in Argentina in general and top-down verticality within the ranks to dismiss his recourse to violence as occurring outside his official capacity: ". . . Esta es una conversación extraoficial"

(35 [This is an unofficial conversation] [30]),[4] or "¡El agente fue herido en servicio: prepárenle una exención médica! (74 [The officer was wounded in the line of duty, get a medical discharge ready] [80]). Evaristo is not above roughing a woman up, either, and it is clear that he is willing to bargain with professional criminals in exchange for information to benefit a higher good (e.g., turning a blind eye to an illegal backroom gambling operation or a business operation based on contraband—and, therefore, perhaps dangerous—medications). Such activities could well be considered to compromise Evaristo's presumed moral commitments, and yet they are the lamentable but understandable cost of pursuing some measure of justice in a country like Argentina, whose historical roots lie in contraband and other illicit business dealings. By refusing to idealize Evaristo, the authors portray in a verisimilar fashion the limitations imposed on moral behavior by the grim realities of a specific social dynamic.

It is important to note that the thirteen stories (six in the English translation) that make up *Evaristo* take place during an indeterminate period in the late 1950s and early 1960s when Argentina is attempting to establish some political continuity between the fall of the Perón presidency and its strong-arm social and economic practices in 1955 and the implantation of the reactionary authoritarian dictatorship in 1966 that will lead, ten years later, to the draconian nightmare of neofascist tyranny (1976–1983); indeed, *Evaristo* is a notable cultural product from the period of the redemocratization of Argentine culture in the period of national reconstruction following the return to constitutionality in late 1983.

There are at least two significant historical references in these stories, aside from the graphic representation of a particular period in Argentine history as revealed by the visible material culture in the strips. The first is Evaristo's trip to Cuba when rebel insurgency has become a problem for urban life—that is, immediately before the January 1959 coup that brought Fidel Castro to power. The other is the thinly veiled story of the capture of Nazi war criminal Adolf Eichmann in the suburbs of Buenos Aires by the Israeli intelligence and security services, the Mossad and the Shin Bet, in June 1960. Usually considered by (at least non-Jewish) Argentines as an outrageous violation of national sovereignty,[5] Israel's actions contributed to the anti-Semitic sentiment that swept Argentina in the 1960s, some of which is evident in *Evaristo.*

There are only two occasions in which Evaristo's attempts fail to sort things out and, circumstantially, effect some moral balance in the world.

C. Sampayo and F. Solano López, *Evaristo*

One is when he fails to prevent his long-lost son from being killed by kidnappers who take advantage of finding out who he is to create an advantage in their favor with the police. Evaristo kills them both before realizing they have already killed his son: he is left never to find out who sent them. The other occasion in which he fails is when he attempts to discover something about the foreign agents spotted in the city (they turn out to be from the Mossad and Shin Bet). He and an associate tail the agents (who are never identified as Israeli—they are only called "the foreigners") and the captured Nazi to the plane they will depart on (presumably to Israel), but they are ambushed by thugs, who beat the two men, leaving Evaristo unconscious.

There is the clear insinuation that elements within the Argentine government and/or armed forces are part of the kidnapping plot. When Evaristo comes to in the hospital, wearing a neck brace, he is informed by the policeman in his room that a military coup has taken place and that the police chief—perhaps ironically, but on whose part?—wishes him a speedy recovery (64 [56]). Meanwhile Evaristo is reading a newspaper, one of whose headlines states: "Los servicios secretos extranjeros actuaron con impunidad, última prueba de corrupción de nuestro gobierno" (64 [The foreign secret service acts with impunity, the ultimate proof of corruption of our government] [56]). However, the much-maligned government of Arturo Frondizi, which came to power in 1958 through indirect elections, is not overthrown by a military coup until March 1962, a couple of months before Eichmann will be hanged for war crimes in Israel (vigorously debated, it was the only time in Israel's history the death penalty was used in a civil case). While the chronological discrepancy might suggest that the allusion is not to the Eichmann case, it is such a notorious breach of Argentine security (made possible, one insists, by internal collaboration) with such serious social and international repercussions that one can hardly understand it to reference a fictional event. Moreover, Evaristo's humiliating failure in his investigations and his own overthrow are pointed objective correlatives of the seriousness of that historical event.

It is, however, important that Sampayo and Solano López's narratives are set in the turbulent but not sharply politically defined period between 1955 and 1966. Had they been set in the Peronista period (1946–1955), Evaristo would have had to assume a political stance vis-à-vis a regime that was populist in nature and putatively socially committed, which would have made him an agent of that period of government and its policies. Certainly, Peronism brought a whole new relationship between the police and the citizenry, particularly the popular classes that most benefited from social-nationalist policies. And although hierarchical corruption undoubtedly prevailed during the period, it is unlikely that the Solano López and Sampayo creative relationship would have wanted to be associated with Peronismo, since the sort of leftist posture they represented found Peronismo's version of socialism false and ineffectual and producing no viable structural change; at the same time, Peronismo had no use for either the old left or any emerging new left and vigorously persecuted whatever it took to be leftist opposition to its policies and programs.

Concomitantly, any identification of Evaristo with the period subsequent to the 1966 coup, which would be the first in a series of seven de facto governments lasting until 1983, would have aligned him with right-wing military interests and the various attempts to realign Argentine order with the prelapsarian history of the country before 1946 and its early fascist past following the pro-Germanic and ultimately pro-Nazi governments that flowed from Argentina's first military coup in 1930. This could hardly have led to the sort of, in the end, sympathetic and, finally, pathetic figure Evaristo is meant to personify. The political turbulence of the end of the 1950s and the beginning of the 1960s is propitious, precisely because it does not lend itself to clear ideological definitions, being fundamentally marked, as in the case of the Frondizi administration from 1958 to 1962, by the—finally futile—attempts to restore a functioning democracy to Argentina.

Indeed, the pathos of the failure of those attempts has, in Evaristo's failures, in the sense of the decline of his once-solid body, and in his bewilderment at times in getting a handle on what is happening out on the street, a secondary effective objective correlative for Argentine social history. This is nowhere more evident than in the story of his failure to save his kidnapped natural son, "Terror en las calles" (Terror in the streets), where his body, beginning to show the signs of irreparable damage from chain smoking, is correlated with that of the aging lion who has escaped from the municipal zoo. The lion, despite public hysteria to the contrary, is no more a threat to the safety of the citizenry than Evaristo's diminishing prowess is a threat to the organized criminals who kill his son. The pathos of this correlation is confirmed when Evaristo, abandoned to the specter of his failure, approaches the lion and pats it on the head, murmuring "Amigo, vos y yo andamos perdidos . . ." (98 [You and I are walking around lost . . . friend . . ."] [102]), and he stares wistfully after the zoo van that disappears down the street, returning the lion to its captivity. And, despite his efforts to give up smoking and to ban smoking around him, his wistfulness is accompanied by a wisp of smoke from the cigarette in his hand.

Solano López, whose most famous artistic collaboration was with Héctor Germán Oesterheld and the latter's *El Eternauta* creation (1957–1959), is marvelously effective with his drawings in capturing the turbulence of this transitional period in Argentine social history and portraying the denizens of the criminal underworld that flourished with that turbulence: Argentina has always had a uniquely abundant underworld, although one could argue that it flourished in particular as a result of the traumatic effects of Peronismo and subsequent attempts, both by military and civilian governments, to counter it. But the center of Solano López's drawings is Evaristo's body, both as formally clothed in his role as police and in various forms of undress, as we see him in his domestic intimacy, in the intimacy of his relations with women, with whom, as befitting the sexism of the period—another touch of brutal realism to counter any possible idealization—Evaristo is not above having sexual relationships for pragmatic as much as personal reasons. Certainly, on several occasions Evaristo is undeniably a cad. We also see him in the intimacy of the Turkish steam bath, trading protection of a notorious contrabandist for information about the missing daughter of a prominent Jewish doctor.

Although Evaristo, in the formal street wear of the day—suit, long-sleeve white shirt, tie, and fedora—comes across as a pudgy functionary, his nearly naked body remains impressive in its virility. We see him as a professional boxer in a flashback, with the hard definition appropriate to the profession, and we see him on at least two subsequent occasions as still a young man, with the solid profile of Clark Kent's conventionally clothed Superman. However, the aging Evaristo, even despite his paunch, is still impressively muscled, retaining a full complement of cranial and bodily hair. We see him sexually active at one point and, although his body is represented as a black silhouette, it is clear from the body language of his partner (here and in other sequences where we are to understand that sex has taken place) that he still performs in quite a satisfactory manner. The woman who has been with him in the scene portrayed in silhouette fashion later attacks another woman whom she believes to be after Evaristo's affections, and the ensuing catfight is a metonym of Evaristo's sustained male potency.

Because of the man's bulk, and note must also be taken of his above-average height, Evaristo dominates the frames in which he appears, often being foregrounded in such a way as to effect this exaggerated perspective. Significantly, we essentially see him standing, and his mere presence is enough to put him in total command of his surroundings, which is why, after he has pointedly punched in the nose a newspaper editor who is complicating his life, it comes across as particularly ironic when he says "No le he pegado, Pérez-Peres" (37 [I didn't hit you, Pérez-Peres] [32]). Evaristo later punches and kicks the man in public and then walks away, brushing his hands off and declaring to the assembled onlookers, "No le he pegado" (43 [I didn't beat him up] [38]), as though saying "I wasn't even here," despite the fashion in which his bodily presence overwhelms everyone else in the frame.[6] Although Evaristo is capable of strong emotion—especially rage in the face of injustice or ineptitude—his face is usually an impassive mask, although we are given to understand in general he doesn't miss a beat, processing details in the depth of his inner being. Perhaps this is the meaning of the added subtitle in the English version of the graphic narrative, *Evaristo*. It is not Buenos Aires as such that is the deep city, although there are undoubtedly many substrata to what is visible in the daily texture of complex Porteño life. But one might postulate that it is Evaristo's probing mind that is the deep city, commensurate in its profundity with the exponentially malevolent evil of the city, both on the part of its hardened criminals and its putatively decent autocracy.

The nature of Evaristo's deep understanding of human motivations that others do not see or do not grasp is evident in the final story, "Leyenda de un pistolero herido" [Legend of a wounded gunman], which turns on a gangster hit man who had forced a doctor to treat him for a gunshot wound. The doctor's attentions are successful but, because he has been coerced into not reporting the incident to the police as required by law, he refuses to accept the gifts his patient attempts to shower him with out of gratitude for having saved his life. Twenty-some years later, the gunman is wounded in a confrontation with the police at which Evaristo is present. He evades the police pursuit, and, dismissing the three agents who accompany him, Evaristo heads straight for the doctor's house, arriving before the wounded gangster. Evaristo arrests him once he has been treated by the doctor. Although Evaristo explains that he surmised that the gangster would once again turn to the doctor who had previously saved his life as the consequence of a relationship of psychological dependency, the doctor can only mutter to himself, with respect to Evaristo, "Ese hombre está loco" (120 [That man's crazy] [111]).

The foregoing parameters of *Evaristo* may be best seen on display in the story "Villa cartón" (Shantytown), in which there is the intersection between violence over a communal water faucet that falls dry in one of the numerous slum areas of Buenos Aires that suddenly rends the close-woven fabric of modernity that in general characterizes the megalopolis, and an apparently psychopathic killer who beats his victims to death with a hammer. In contrast with Evaristo's efforts to discover both who is responsible for the disruption of water distribution and who is responsible for the brutal killings, one of the local newspapers undertakes to exploit the sensationalist nature of the crime to the maximum, stressing his nature as a "loco" (madman). One of the frames (69 [75]) shows a front page with a screaming headline and identifies the paper as *La Razón*, a legendary evening tabloid that appealed to populist working class sentiments and interests.[7] Needless to say, the point is that such sensationalism and the hysteria it provokes—who is this madman and who is his next victim and why?—only interferes with the search for the truth, since it is dedicated to creating an alternative reality that serves manipulatively to sell newspapers, an alternative reality based on a narrative logic significantly at odds with what Evaristo grounds his investigation in. If Evaristo's procedure is based on establishing in a rational fashion the relationship between objective evidence at his disposal—the classical motivating force of detective fiction, inspired by a privileged prowess of deduction—the narrative logic of the newspaper is animated by maximizing selective points and attributing meaning to them as dictated by the imperative to be sensationalist; that there is less of a perceived coherence between the points than both a disregard for coherence and even a prizing of a rhetorically useful incoherence matters little or nothing to the nature of yellow journalism. Where it becomes something other than commercially motivated noise in the background is when it ends up undercutting Evaristo's socially legitimate police investigation, especially when we learn that there is a direct relationship between the brutal murders and the despair-inducing circumstance of the curtailment of water distribution to the shantytown.

This is so because the narrative Evaristo ends up discovering, rather than really elaborating in the tradition of the deduction-driven investigator, is that the murders are the work of someone apparently from the shantytown, although his identity is never really confirmed. After Evaristo discovers, almost by chance, who is ultimately responsible for the curtailment of water in the slum (again, it is not really clear why the head of Water Resources curtails the water supply, but one can assume it is more profitable, illegally, to divert it elsewhere), the so-called madman beats the head of Water Resources to death with a hammer and then turns himself in to the police. The narrative is not directly interested in the workings of police procedure nor in the subsequent legal process the murderer will be forced to endure. Rather, the interest lies with the circumstances of the slum and the intertwined precariousness of human existence there and the likely permanence of its reality for those who are also forced to endure it by the socioeconomic realities of the country.

Evaristo is, in the end, nothing more than a hapless bystander, unable to do anything about what he witnesses, investigates, analyzes, and acts on within the very constrained parameters of his official position. Unlike an American comic-book hero or the action figure of a Hollywood film, Evaristo is helpless, as he can neither be much of an enforcer nor, unlike his Batman urban counterparts, an agent of significant justice. In this way, his official narrative is decidedly pathetic, and one understands why the outrageously falsified narratives of the newspaper, which at one point goes so far as to stage one of the murders to provide illustrative material for its story, are able to have seductively engaged a readership: although, despite doing so in an unwitting fashion, Evaristo "solves" this case, he has no engaging "real" narrative to offer in place of the newspaper's, being content only to learn that, mysteriously, water service, with the death of the man who controlled it, has been restored to the slum. When he utters the final words of the narrative with reference to a group of boys playing soccer (the diagonal here corresponds to a pull back to pan the slum, with his final word off in a corner as an inconsequential tag), the graphic artist signals that there is nothing more to do or say, and we know Evaristo will simply move on to one more criminal situation in a never-ending succession of police crises: "No saldrán nunca de aquí . . . / . . . nunca" (82 [They'll never get out of here . . . / . . . never] [88]).

Evaristo is finally done in both by the overarching corruption of the Argentine system and by his own penchant for cutting corners, no matter how justified. As he presents a judge with a dossier of evidence in a case he has been pursuing, he is informed that he is under arrest as the consequence of accusations against him and is ordered arrested. The closing image of *Evaristo* is the tearing up by the judge of the dossier Evaristo has just submitted to him and tossing it into the trash can

C. Sampayo and F. Solano López, *Evaristo*

(196). This particularly graphic representation of his downfall ensures our understanding that, in the end, whatever Evaristo stands for morally and ethically is no match for sociohistorical realities that are as unmovable and intransigent as those ranged against the young shantytown dwellers he attempts to defend.

Indeed, there is an almost nostalgic note to Sampayo and Solano López's evocation of the legendary Evaristo Meneses, a sense of a prelapsarian Argentina in which, although perhaps to call them noble figures might have been an exaggeration, there was some level of mutual respect between the citizenry and the police, a sense that it might just be possible for representatives of the latter to be respectable and reputable human beings. Whether or not the highly professionalized police force that predominates in post-tyranny Buenos Aires enjoys the support of the people is a matter for sociological inquiry. The real sense of *Evaristo*, however, is what was lost with the absorption of the police force into the regime of terror that gripped Argentine society after 1976, in which the sort of highly individualized and often profoundly machista[8] yet morally grounded policing of someone like Evaristo became forever superseded.

CHAPTER 5

News Bulletins from the Gender Wars: Patricia Breccia's *Sin novedad en el frente*

Hay muchas historias en la ciudad desnuda, y ésta, aunque no lo parezca, . . . es una de ellas.
[There are a lot of stories in the naked city, and this one, although it might not seem to be, . . . is one of them.]
BRECCIA 74

Patricia Breccia (1955–) is unquestionably the best of a rather minuscule inventory of women engaged in graphic narrative or in the broad arena of the comics.[1] While this is not the place to explore the masculinism of the genre, it is readily apparent that women have either not been drawn to the genre or have been unsuccessful in emerging as major voices.[2] Only Argentina's Maitena (nom de plume[3] of Maitena Burundanera [1962–]) has had a mass audience—and, despite her successes in publishing in newspapers and journals and in collecting her work into best-selling volumes, she has abandoned the graphic format in recent years, turning to more conventional (and excellent) traditional literary narratives (see Tompkins's important study on Maitena). Although it is the case that Maitena prospered with single-panel texts, or various panels and strips arranged into an artistic statement on rarely more than one page, the boundaries between her microtexts and larger narrative elaborations are tenuous and arbitrary at best, and there is much in her work to satisfy the demanding definitions of both the graphic and the narrative.

Breccia, who has developed an artistic persona pronouncedly different from that of her father—Alberto Breccia (1919–1993),[4] one of the founding giants of a sophisticated comic art that allowed for the transition to the distinctive differences of the graphic narrative—has pub-

P. Breccia, *Sin novedad en el frente*

lished in some of the major graphic forums in Argentina, like the fabled *Humor registrado*; its more "intellectual" counterpart *Superhumor*;
and its successor *Fierro*, among others.[5] One of her most successful creations, in the early 1980s, was the feminist strip *Sol de Noche* [Nighttime
sun], on which she collaborated with novelist Guillermo Saccomanno.[6]

In all of her work, Breccia has strived to give a hard-edged representation of the difficulties of being a woman, particularly an independent and strong-willed woman, in Buenos Aires.[7] This is not a matter of the problems of self-realization for women under military tyranny (1976–1983) versus constitutional democracy (post-1983), although there can be little doubt that the masculinist armed forces enhanced the layers and levels of frustration for women who sought self-determination and self-realization. Breccia[8] could be understood as a feminine version of Raúl Scalabrini Ortiz, especially as regards his now famous essay on *El hombre que está solo y espera* ([The man who stands waiting alone] 1931). Indeed, the cover of Mercader's novel shows a woman seated alone at a café table, smoking and staring out the window at the street; it is typical of the humble neighborhood variety of such cafés of which there must be thousands throughout the city of Buenos Aires—sometimes three to four on the corners of an intersection, even in the most modest reaches of the streets. Martha Mercader's novel *Solamente ella* (1982) carries, below the photograph in question, a publicity pitch: "Ser mujer en la Argentina, pavada de proyecto" (It's a cockamamie idea to even think of being a woman in Argentina). Breccia's characters, Sol de Noche in the eponymous work with Saccomanno and her unnamed women in *Sin novedad en el frente*, represent the Argentine adjectives *histérica, loca, nerviosa* [hysterical, crazy, upset], which meld into each other as a shifting and overdetermined constellation of deprecating characterizations of women who speak up, speak out, and speak back.[9]

Furthermore, Breccia, who writes her own texts in *Sin novedad,*[10] draws women who are exuberant, loud, flamboyant, in-your-face, excessive, and uncontrolled—women who are drawn often with flowing hair that fills in spaces in the panels, with hips, breasts, and gestures that accomplish the same. The balloons of their speech may overwhelm a panel, if it is not the death-ray vibes emanating from their eyes. Moreover, since many of Breccia's stories take place at night, the landscape is dominated by a grotesque and contorted moon, of course an anchor symbol of womanhood; like Breccia's women, the moon also tends to dominate the graphic panel.[11] I would suggest that the best characterization of Breccia's style is expressionistic, as she strives to represent the inner turmoil and frustration of women checkmated at every turn by a hostile male environment and as she strives to detail the range of women's reactions to the circumstances of their environment in what is rather like a sampler of the most extreme forms of neuroses, psychoses, and schizophrenia.

P. Breccia, *Sin novedad en el frente*

The land mines are everywhere for both the independent woman and the (relatively) submissive one, since part of the sense of the battlefield women traverse that is portrayed here is that there is no way of getting it right, no way to disarm the land mines or to protect oneself from them. Breccia goes to considerable length to sustain the battlefield metaphor for her universe of Argentine existential experience, including the recurring use of the top-of-the-page banner "Parte de Guerra" (War Bulletin) with multiple variations. Both tumultuous action and an externalized psychic turmoil are the basis for the often grim and always trenchant conjunctions of text and image that make up the eleven short stories that constitute *Sin novedad en el frente,* a title that echoes several major narrative tropes (most specifically Erich Maria Remarque's 1929 World War I novel, *Im Westin nichts Neues,* translated into English as *All Quiet on the Western Front,* and filmed in both 1930 and 1979 under this title),[12] as well as articulating pithily that nothing changes for women.[13] This can clearly be seen by no substantive difference in the representation of women's lives between *Sol de Noche,* drawn under the military dictatorship, and *Sin novedad en el frente,* drawn well into the return to constitutional democracy.

The grotesque expressionistic detail abounds in Breccia's texts, creating an overwhelming redundancy of meaning as regards a female existential stance. First, there are the graphic details I have mentioned, which I will discuss in greater detail as I examine some selected stories. But there is also the matter of the lettering used for both the dialogue balloons and narrative transitions. The norm in comic-book art is to use tidy capital block letters, enhanced rhetorically by boldface, typesize increase, and affective punctuation marks as the narrativized situation might demand. Even a distinctively expressionistic artist like Robert Crumb makes use of lettering that presents no significant challenge as regards intelligibility. However, Breccia's lettering is markedly iconoclastic. In addition to deviating significantly from a strictly linear progression of letters, Breccia may shift typefaces from simple lines to virtual scrawls and from simple lines to enhancements such as shadowing and outlining. Letters may overlap and the parallel lines of letters like "m" and "n" may become splayed, while the overlapping of letters may be accompanied by a notable variation from the plumb line of the conventional font case. The effect, when self-expression and dialogue are at issue, is the psychic decentering associated with a traumatic state, and when interior monologue is at issue, to express the inner turmoil of the individual.

When a disembodied narrative voice is involved, the result is a pattern of recompilation and foreshadowing of the extreme states of existential being experienced by the women protagonists of the stories. In one opening panel, a woman wakes up at four in the morning. Tears stain her face and she sits up in bed, clutching a closed fist to her chest, where her heart is beating wildly. The lettering, divided into three lines that head the three single-image strips depicting this event, reads: "Cuatro de la mañana, hora en que los ángeles cuentan pequeñas historias de amores endiablados . . . / . . . oscura hora donde las mujeres tontas se dedican a volar por las ventanas . . . / . . . y en la que ciertos corazones pierden, como cañerías rotas . . ." (45).[14] The page is headed by the banner "Sin novedad en el frente" and the recurring logo, above the final letters of "frente," the English phrase "hepatics minds." This phrase is rather incoherent, both because "hepatic" (of, relating to, or affecting the liver) is an incongruous modifier for the abstract noun "minds," with the intent, presumably, of engendering a metaphoric construction: minds, as though a concrete human organ, characterized by the processes or, perhaps, the diseases of the liver, such as cirrhosis. Secondly, Breccia has endowed the noun phrase (NP [Adj N]) with the morphosyntax of Spanish whereby the adjective agrees in number (but not grammatical gender, which, of course, English basically lacks) with the head noun. This incongruous and solecistic feature of this logo recurs as part of the opening banner of many of the eleven stories and serves as an icon of the disturbed decentering of the existential being of women as portrayed in *Sin novedad en el frente*.

The third story in the collection, "Hoy: el abuelo de la nada" [Today, the grandfather of nothingness] underscores the urban solitude of women, while at the same time their willingness to be at the service of the equally lonely men, but with the difference that the latter have an agency the former lack. The opening panel sets the stage: "Noche, telón de fondo . . . Afuera hacía más frío que un amor en déficit . . ." ([Night as the backdrop . . . It's colder outside than a relationship in the red] 29). Presided over by a delirious-looking face of the moon, a psychedelic vision of the Buenos Aires cityscape narrows to a decrepit apartment in which a leaking faucet drips in a kitchen sink piled with dirty dishes and an equally disorderly bathroom in which the cockroaches perform a song and dance routine, only subsequently to be splotched by a rabid kitty named Fantomas Trigger. Our unkempt heroine is sprawled on her bed reading one of Crumb's comic books when the telephone rings. She answers to an anonymous declaration of love and, after listening to a string of incoherences, she slams the phone down with the interjection "¡Imbécil!" ([Imbecile!] 30). While such calls may not represent immediate physical threats, they are nevertheless a psychological violation of individual privacy. Given the statistics of anonymous violence toward women, those who receive such calls—especially those who live alone—justifiably feel violated. The narrator dismisses the incident: "La noche no daba para más: un puñado de locos mirándose al espejo. . ." ([That was all the night was good for: a handful of crazies looking at themselves in the mirror] 31).[15]

Our heroine returns to her issue of Crumb but is interrupted again, this time by the ringing of her doorbell rather than the phone. This time her privacy is literally invaded by an aged grandfatherly type, who, as he leans on his cane, announces that he is an old poet who died the night before and is looking for a bit of refuge and a warm cup of tea in order to complete a poem he left unfinished when he died. The moon exclaims "Oh!" and a serpent, the urban descendant of the prototype of sin in the Garden of Eden, utters "¡Grooakkk!" as though a cry of warning.[16]

Taking pity on the avuncular stranger, our heroine seats him comfortably in an armchair and prepares him a warming cup of tea. He makes his request: "Necesito una noche, la suya, y una mesa . . . ¿Usted tiene? . . . Para terminar mi poema . . ." ([I need one night, yours, and a table . . . Do you have one? . . . To finish my poem] 33). He thereupon recites a supposedly incomplete text: "¿Qué inmenso pájaro nocturno[,] qué silenciosa pluma total neutral . . .? [What immense bird of the night, what totally neutral silent plume?], which is a text from the Spanish Nobel poet Vicente Aleixandre's *Sombra del paraíso* ([Shadow of paradise] 1944), which is also where the lines uttered by the anonymous phone caller come from (the latter is given in an asterisked note, but the former is not). Deciding to leave him alone with his postmortem task, our heroine goes out into the busy Porteño night, where she seeks out a volume of poetry: it is not made clear how she knows how to find it—one of the many purposeful narrative inconsistencies in Breccia's stories. When she discovers that the poem is, in fact, a complete text, she returns to her apartment, where she finds a note taped to the armchair in which the elderly man begs her to forgive him for his deception, that he is really not a dead poet, but "solo un viejo que necesitaba pasar una última noche, con un último recuerdo: usted" ([only an old man who needed to spend one last night, with one last memory: you] 34). In the final panel, in an interesting exercise of pathetic fallacy, the moon speaks as though articulating the woman's resignation to the course of events: "La noche caía a raudales, era una lluvia negra, pero no ensuciaba . . . Me fui a dormir . . . por hoy, no quería más visitas" ([Night fell in bunches, it was a black rain, but it didn't make you dirty . . . I went to bed . . . at least for today I wanted no more visitors] 34). Taking Fantomas Trigger in her arms, she clicks off the light and the strip goes black with a final panel.

There is something creepy about all this, especially since the woman has been a double victim of the psychological invasion of her privacy, first by an anonymous phone call and then by an unidentified stranger. Both events are linked by the use of Aleixandre's poetry, which was characterized by its concern over sadness, human fellowship, and spiritual unity, although none of the latter two really takes place in this text, and if sadness is a part of urban anomie that may mark the lives of all three characters (the woman as victim and her two inopportune visitors) it is only an uncharacterized background coloring. Grim solitude would seem to be more the ambience at issue here, as conveyed by the grimaces of the moon. In both cases, the woman is exploited by her visitor, first by being obliged to listen to a declaration of love which, if penned by Aleixandre, is uttered by a stranger whose call she has not authorized, and then by the elderly man, who really doesn't get her company, since she leaves him alone to allow him to finish his poem. Thus his company is in reality a sort of a set of fetishes in the form of the details of her apartment, her personal items (including the cat), and any smell or aura she leaves behind as she exits to leave him alone. He evokes this set of fetishes by implication when he utters the English-language cliché: "¡Ah! ¡Home Sweet Home!" (31) when his entrance invades her space uninvited and unannounced.

What is notable about our heroine's reaction is that she appears basically resigned to such invasions, which only serves to enhance the sense of creepiness that is the particular affect of this and other strips: these women may experience anger and frustration, but on the whole they are unable to do much more than accept the circumstances of their existential being. Here, as a final gesture, the woman turns off the light and goes to bed with her cat, as though all in a night's routine.

Two of the stories, however, do show women engaged in the agentive act of suicide, a rather horrendous way of taking charge of one's own life and body. In the first story, "Naturaleza muerta" [Still life] suicide is the response to a culmination of indignities and interrogations about them that lead to no viable answers. The reaction of one of the Buenos Aires machos of the night, who are the protagonists of her torment, is conclusive in dismissing the inconsequence of her self-drowning. The narrator asks: "¿Que [*sic*] va a pensar el hombre, las veredas, las calles . . . . . . los baldíos, las tierras cenagosas, los patios, el vestíbulo . . ." ([What must man, the sidewalks, the streets . . . . . . the vacant lots, the patches of muddy ground, the patios, the entrance ways be thinking?] 18), to which the prototypic denizen of all these realms responds: "Sí . . . otra estúpida mofeta vieja . . ." ([Yes . . . another old skunk of a woman] 18). The final line, however, belongs to the narrator, but as a vain rhetorical question: "¿Qué va a pensar, ahora, el qué dirán?" ([What will the gossip think now?] 18). Indeed.

The ninth story is titled "Sin novedad en el frente: 'nada personal'" [No news from the front: nothing personal] and centers on the same nameless heroine of "El abuelo de la nada." The opening strip once again features a grotesquely visaged moon, but this time one that is explicitly female in that its surface also contains breasts and what appears to be a vagina. Elsewhere in the collection, the moon is not specifically marked for gender, other than the way in which the grammatical gender of the Spanish noun "luna" enables the metaphoric projection of female identity and female affect for the moon. Since the moon presides over many of the texts, engaging often in a relationship of pathetic fallacy with what is transpiring below in the urban spaces of Buenos Aires, it is reasonable to assume that Breccia means for the moon to be understood as a physical world correlative of female experience. In "Nada personal," however, the representation of primary and secondary sexual characteristics renders the correlation unmistakable. The banner along the top of the strip, enunciated either by a disembodied third-person narrator or by the moon itself, states "'Ella' está ahí, hoy. No le pasa nada en especial" (["She's" there today. Nothing special is happening to her] 77).

The use of "nada" in both the title of the story and in this opening banner is multiply ambiguous. Does the absence of anything special signal that the woman's life is uneventful? If so, that would serve to deny the validity of executing a narrative about it, since, as a consequence, there would be nothing to tell. Or, does it mean that, qua woman, there is nothing happening in her life because, typically, she is marginalized from whatever the purportedly real business of life is—i.e., those things that men do and cause to happen to them? If this were the case, then the narrative justification would lie in the imperative to record the circumstances and processes of women's marginalization, the ways in which she does not count for anything in what is alleged to be the mainstream of human existence. Or, finally, does it mean the Sartrean nothingness of her life is a deep psychic scar? This would not be, then, the blank slate of anonymous nonexistence, but rather the deep anguish of a life consciousness of the nothingness that characterizes it and without any possibility of relieving the ache of nothingness with substantive or meaningful being. It is a being in the world that is chokingly restricted by the absence of doing in the world: a human being radically and utterly extraneous to the movement of life around it.

Breccia characterizes her character here as gripped with discomfort ("incómoda' [77]), as though weighed down by a wet pullover, unsettled by the shadows of her apartment, but as insensitive to the light as a blind person. Subsequent panels represent her body in fragments, bleeding on occasion off the page, as though the decentered and cropped graphic representation were the expression of her psychic disconnectedness. The accompanying text is replete with direct or indirect subjunctives that signal this disconnectedness and how to maybe get beyond it. A summation of her situation might, in another context, read as a pastoral idyll of the letting go of the pressures and harriedness of life, of, as the cliché goes, "being in the moment," released from any urgency to be out conquering the world: ". . . Pero en realidad . . . No pasa nada, solo el aullido del tren, la luna mirando algunas cosas, la plaza intacta bajo esos focos espantados . . . O el rumor de algún gato que camina en voz baja" (79).[17] This panorama is almost Zen-like in what might be for others a sought-after placidness in a moment of refuge from the urban madness. But the text receives the rejoinder ". . . Nada más . . ." [. . . Nothing else . . .] from a drunken derelict about to pass out on the sidewalk, being sniffed by the softly murmuring cat. Such an image is hardly Zen-like, and it contradicts the suggested idyllic nature of the text as to how there are no spiritual refuges in the urban landscape, which is relentlessly populated with the detritus of human life and drained of any beneficent poetic feeling. The drunk's "Nada más" is echoed by the protagonist, who, if she is not chain smoking, is gripping her coffee cup with the strawberry design: nicotine and caffeine appear to be her only forms of sentient stimulation.

Halfway through this narration of a woman's experience of life as a meaningless void, there is the banner "2do parte de guerra | 11 p.m. | domingo" ([2nd bulletin of the war | 11 p.m. | Sunday] 80). This news bulletin from the urban front would seem to announce that there is something to report or that there has been a change in the situation. But true to the overarching title of the collection, everything remains totally quiet, mortally quiet. Rather, in place of any information about change, the narrator's indirect discourse of the woman's inner states once again returns to the subjunctive mode, this time colored by the higher predicate "Quisiera que" ([I wish that] 80) and later the conditional "Si" ([If] 81). Suddenly her morose and jumbled thoughts are interrupted by a commotion out on the street, and we are shown the extended feet of a woman lying on her side. Then there comes a banging at her door: it is the police, who inform her that her neighbor has committed suicide by jumping from the balcony of her apartment, and did she know her? They leave when she answers she only knew her as much as she knows herself (82), which is not strictly true, since early on we see her greeting her neighbor across their adjacent balconies. She then goes out on the balcony to view the scene for herself.

The final strip of four panels is really quite artistically effective in conveying something like the communicating vessels of the mind with her neighbor. There is a text distributed across the four panels. Panel 1: Smoking, she seems to look inward and says "Es así nomás . . ." [That's the way it is . . .]; panel 2: A woman is seen lying sprawled on the sidewalk, partially covered by some pages of a newspaper: ". . . Cuando no pasa nada . . ." [When nothing happens]; panel 3: We see the upper torso of the woman, also partially covered by a newspaper, but we also see that her breasts are similar in shape to the protagonist's, and she is also wearing a simple bracelet on her right wrist[18]; now she is lying on her back: ". . . A cierta gente . . . [Some people]; panel 4: As though a camera moving up the woman's body, the final take is now of her entire upper torso, and we see that it is now the protagonist of the story, her eyes opening with the same absent inward look: ". . . Se da por matarse . . ." ([She's into killing herself] 82).

Suicide remains a taboo in Argentina and is formally illegal, which allows for the subjects of unsuccessful attempted suicide to be remanded as wards of the state, subject accordingly to involuntary psychiatric treatment. But to be sure, suicide is a form of doing, a form of taking control over one's body, if at least in only the most transitory and final of fashions, producing an irreversible cessation of the pain of being, whether psychological or physical. The "Fin" [End] at bottom of panel 4 is unquestionably a semantic reduplication here.

One of the characteristics of Breccia's graphic narratives involves the deployment of ambiguity such that the reader is left not really being sure of what has happened. We do know that an act of suicide has taken place, but is one woman involved or are there two deaths, the second being a spur-of-the-moment copycatting of the neighbor's suicide? We

P. Breccia, *Sin novedad en el frente*

seem to see two bodies positioned differently, one on its side, one on its back, with the latter clearly the protagonist of the story, with her face, bracelet, and, it would seem, breasts. Yet, there is a variation in hairstyles. At times throughout the narrative, it would seem that two women are sharing the same story, one with a blonde pageboy cut and one with abundant black curly locks, like the neighbor she greeted early on across their adjacent balconies, even if the latter, who is shown lying on the sidewalk, matches the former in significant details. It would seem to be that two neighbors, isolated from each other (the one says she does not know the other) experience the same radical anomie and commit similar suicides. This is, then, the meaning of the story's title "Nada personal": it is a story that does not affect one person in particular, but rather a class of persons, presumably women on their own in the urban desert, which well might explain why the ostensible protagonist has no name and is identified only as "Ella": these women are interchangeable, both on the basis of their profound existential despair and on the basis of how they respond to it: no other clarification of narrative details is required, since the story is, in effect, nothing personal.

The stories in *Sin novedad en el frente* all, with one exception ("Malapata" [Bad news], which involves an evangelical preacher, one of the macho doers of the urban landscape), involve women like the three I have characterized in this commentary. They are representative, like Breccia's earlier Sol de Noche, of the woman in her twenties on her own in the harsh Porteño environment. Whether their existential despair is extendable to all women in Buenos Aires, or in Argentina, is questionable, although there is certainly the conventional narrative record to support how it effectively can be: even a conventional, highly conservative male writer like Eduardo Mallea (1903–1982), in his novels set mostly in the 1940s and 1950s, was interested in capturing the silent despair of both men and women (e.g., the female protagonist of his *Todo verdor perecerá* [1943]). What is important is not, however, the sociological validation of Breccia's "narrative sample" nor the way in which perhaps some of the feminist issues she explores are today, two decades later and with significant feminist activity in Argentina, very well established. Rather it lies in the firmly innovative control she has over her artistic medium, the often bizarre nature of her expressionistic graphics and the often disconcerting nature of her use of verbal texts, especially with their unconventional lettering practices. But taken in conjunction as a whole, Breccia's work is distinctively original, as original as was her father's, and unquestionably a solid point of reference for women's (still minuscule) intervention in the graphic narrative genre.[19] To be sure, what is important is not that the author of this material is a woman, but that, in a field in which masculinist points of view dominate so insistently, the presence of a female character with concerns and interests that can properly be characterized as feminine and feminist is especially welcome.

PART II

BRAZIL: GRAPHIC NARRATIVE AS POSTMODERN AND GLOBALIZED CONSCIOUSNESS

CHAPTER 6

Of Death and the Road:
Rafael Grampá's *Mesmo Delivery*

The mash-and-slash graphic novel by Rafael Grampá (birth date unavailable), *Mesmo Delivery* (2008)[1] is principally interesting because of a mystery that is central to its action, the nature of the cargo ex-boxer Rufo and his sidekick Sangrecco are carrying for Mesmo Delivery. We never learn what that cargo is, although the mash-and-slash mayhem that takes place at a truck stop seems somehow to have something to do with the cargo. The fact that Sangrecco may know what the cargo is—or is to be—and that he somehow engineers its fulfillment enhances narrative interest by deepening the mystery of the cargo.

Mesmo Delivery consists of a chronologically arranged main narrative line and four flashbacks, one of which refers to Rufo being KO-ed in a fight and three that take place in Mesmo Delivery's dispatch office (one in which Rufo is hired and two in which his sidekick is given separate orders by the dispatcher). In these flashbacks, we learn that Rufo is an ex-boxer who has never driven a big rig before and that his sidekick cannot drive but has been sent along to comply with separate orders from the dispatcher. Although the nature of the cargo is never identified, we learn that it involves nine of something, the biggest request the company has received so far (52). Subsequently, we learn that the driver, Rufo, is part of the shipment (56). All of this piques Sangrecco's interest and he agrees to be discreet about the shipment. The reader's interest, however, is piqued when Sangrecco reacts to the indication that Rufo is to know nothing about the cargo by arguing that how, then, is he supposed "to get these folks down the road in the truck without the driver catching on?" (52).

The main narrative line of the novel involves Rufo's need to take advantage of a truck stop to use the bathroom. When he goes on to request a glass of milk from the man who tends the counter, the contrast between his hulking frame and the choice of beverage arouses the derision of the three men and two women who occupy one of the stop's booths. Spoiling for a fight, one of the men, egged on by the other four, provokes Rufo with taunts that both infantilize him and question his sexuality. Rufo, counting on his size and the scrawny look of the other, thinks he will have an easy time subduing the ratty-looking would-be opponent. But the latter exchanges what looks like a normal right fist for a larger-than-life prosthetic that appears to be made of cement. This allows the provocateur to deliver a quick haymaker to Rufo that leaves him out cold on the ground. With Rufo out of the way, the victor thinks he will supplement his pugilistic triumph by looting the truck of its cargo.

Without recounting the successive scenes of mayhem, suffice it to say that the five individuals who occupied the booth at the truck stop when Rufo arrived end up, in quick succession, dead. All three men are killed by Sangrecco, along with one of the prostitutes, while Rufo kills the other prostitute by mistake when he comes to and attempts to knock out his provocateur, who picks him up and hurls him through the truck stop's plate glass window, leaving him once again out cold. Sangrecco then proceeds to kill the truck-stop employee, who has attempted to call the police. Sangrecco packs the truck with the five dead bodies, as the salivating Devil rubs his hands in contentment from his subterranean cave (47).[2] The reader by this point will have guessed that the cargo Mesmo Delivery traffics in is dead bodies and that the Devil, or his terrestrial agent, has contracted the cargo. Sangrecco, it turns out, is not just Rufo's nondriving sidekick, sent along to accompany the new man on the job to see he does things right, such as abiding by orders not to open the cargo bin. Rather, Sangrecco's responsibility is to produce the cargo, presumably by killing people along the way to complete the requisite unit specification of the cargo. When the man who knocks Rufo out forces the door of the cargo bin open, he is greeted by Sangrecco, who, wielding carved butcher knives, severs his head. It plops at the foot of his four companions, three of whom Sangrecco will proceed to deal with in the same fashion. The body count is now six (the five inhabitants of the truck stop's booth and the counter attendant) and, since the dispatcher has assured Sangrecco that Rufo will become part of the cargo, it is only a matter of time until he joins the heap of bodies in the cargo bin as one of the three remaining units of the consignment.

Mesmo Delivery does not explain how the consignment is completed

R. Grampá, *Mesmo Delivery*

R. Grampá, *Mesmo Delivery*

or delivered. Rufo comes to and rejoins Sangrecco in the cab, who has cleaned up the killing ground and acts as if he has never left the cab during Rufo's absence. The strip concludes as they proceed on their way, accompanied by a raven who flies over the truck with a tooth in its mouth (Rufo's?) picked up from the ground where the massacre took place.

The mystery of the cargo may be clarified by the reader's coming to understand that Mesmo Delivery traffics in dead bodies. But it deepens in the absence of two items of further information. One relates to the function of those bodies. Although Brazil has had its share of cases involving trafficking in contraband human organs, dead bodies transported piled on top of each other in the cargo bin of a cross-country big rig in a semi-tropical country like Brazil are useless for organ transplants, and the matter is left open as to what the purpose of hauling dead bodies as freight might be. I will return to this matter in a moment.

The second unexplained detail is where the additional bodies will come from. We know that Rufo's is to be added to the initial harvest of six cadavers, and presumably the other two will come from one or another of the further stops along the road. Perhaps Sangrecco is destined to join his own cargo. There is, thus, an irony in his being entertained by how Rufo is transporting himself as cargo (56), since he in turn may be engaged in transporting himself as additional cargo. This leaves one consigned unit unaccounted for, and this leaves the reader (who, as I will explain in a moment, is given an interior duplication in the novel) as the final unit that will complete the cargo.

While this suggestion might seem too pat, it is important to consider what Grampá may be undertaking to represent with *Mesmo Delivery*. I would suggest that, on one general existentialist level, he is referring to the act of living as a journey toward death, a trope that is highlighted by the use of the framework of cross-country trucking.[3] In this sense, Mesmo Delivery crisscrosses the countryside transporting dead bodies (for the Devil?) as a metaphor for the way in which the traffic and commerce of life is a journey toward death, as much inevitable for Rufo as it is for the cargo he otherwise unwittingly hauls. Death, customarily violent, is only a matter of the accidental circumstances of the road, such as requesting a glass of milk within earshot of a group spoiling for a fight.

Yet there is more of an allegorical dimension to Grampá's story, since Mesmo Delivery's road trip takes place in anything but an idyllic setting. In addition to contributing itself to environmental pollution, the rig moves through an industrial wasteland that the trucking industry in part serves (the other part it serves is the consumerist urban concentrations whose much-vaunted standard of living depends on the goods the trucks haul). Many of Brazil's truck stops are found in natural settings (some quite lush in the south and in the Amazonian region), where the only thing disrupting the natural setting is the highway and the stops along it. But Grampá's vision is of a bleak and forbidding wasteland (see, especially, the images on p. 11), and the truck stops are grimy joints with nonfunctioning toilet facilities. Grampá takes particular delight in representing the unappealing nature of the truck stop, which, with the array of signs and displays in English, really looks more like the decaying remnants of US gas stations of almost a hundred years ago, in the fashion of Ed Ruscha's concept photography. Grampá appears to particularly delight in the kitsch nostalgia of such establishments, as in the case of the full-page throwback American advertisements he reproduces (48–49).

In this fashion, Grampá's portrayal of a Brazilian road trip diverges from Paulo Thiago's Everyman film *Jorge, um brasileiro* (1989), with its paean to the rugged individual who embodies the best of Brazilian take-charge manhood and the ability to get done what has to be done out of solidarity with his fellow social subjects. Mesmo Delivery is part of the problem, not the opportunity for the beneficent Everyman to show his mettle. Rather Mesmo Delivery is part of the environmental decay that both augments and is augmented by the insouciantly violent individuals that populate the landscape where, to the delight of the Devil, murderous death comes sooner than expected. Graphic narrative has made almost a fetish out of relating interpersonal violence to a decaying social condition portrayed in the most ghoulish fashion possible, and Grampá's work is no exception. If Rufo is to be one of the unsuspecting victims of his new occupation, why would Sangrecco or even the reader be any exception: in all, the nine victims requested, and the consignment is complete.

From a graphic point of view, Rufo's body dominates the frames in which it appears, easily larger than the other six bodies he runs into at the truck stop combined. But unlike Thaigo's Jorge, whose imposing beefcake body dominates the frames of *Jorge, um brasileiro* in contrast to the often squalid bodies of individuals whose lives he assists,[4] Rufo is anything but an Everyman, as prone to bloody battle as his provocateurs are. Indeed, he kills one of the two prostitutes with a misdirected left-handed hook aimed at the man who had KO-ed him.

One of the narrative features of *Mesmo Delivery* is the internal representation of spectatorship. Certainly, the reader/audience is always the essential spectator of cultural production, and the semiotic processes of the text are oriented toward complying with the witnessing of life that cultural production appeals to, especially when visual art overtly "frames" the spectacle for us readers. Moreover, Grampá's full utilization of all of the possibilities for magnifying the frame in order to highlight specific actions and events is designed to overwhelm the reader to the greatest possible affective extent. When internal duplication of spectatorship is involved, the text becomes even more explicit as regards what we are supposed to be witnessing.

Thus, as Rufo and the five individuals who have taunted him move outside to play out the violent drama they have set in motion, the counter attendant takes a seat, literally, at the picture window, as though it were a giant television or movie screen, cigarette in hand, to witness the action. The way in which that action will intrude on the spectator (and thus, by implication, on the reader as the external spectator, framed by the boundaries of the physical object of the book being read) when Rufo is thrown through the window, and the way in which the attendant himself will become the sixth unit of cargo, has resonance for any idea real-world readers might feel or wish to hold themselves as separate from the violence the graphic novel is displaying. Circumstantially, Rufo's provocateur's companions are multiple internal witnesses to the violence their taunts set in motion in a way in which Sangrecco is not: he knows that something will likely take place—doesn't it always in places like this truck stop?—and he only need step in at a later point to execute his role and clean up the mess, which means depositing the bodies in the cargo bin of the truck. Other internal spectators are the raven, the black bird of death, who carries off as a talisman the knocked-out tooth that is a keepsake of the operation, and, of course, the Devil himself, whose satanic needs, in the end, appear to be what all of this grim display of lived human experience is designed to satisfy.

There is a measure of irony in Sangrecco's delight at Rufo's being unaware that he is part of the cargo at issue here. But there that irony is written large by the very name of the trucking company that gives its name to Grampá's novel, *Mesmo Delivery*. The English-language translation does not attempt to translate this name/title; perhaps the feeling was that the result would be too clumsily noncolloquial in English. In Portuguese, *mesmo* means "self," as in *eu mesmo*, "I myself." It can also be used as a phatic marker and, when used in response to something that has been said, means something like "right on," "you can say that again," "you got that right," and similar such formulas. But as an emphatic particle, it is used with nouns to underscore their uniqueness; as a reflexive participle, it is used to implicate the subject as complement to the action being described. Thus, even when the title of Grampá's novel uses the word "delivery" in the original Portuguese,[5] the title *Mesmo Delivery* can be read as a "delivery service of/for/by one's self." Such an understanding would fit in with what Rufo does not know: that he himself is going to be part of the cargo he is hauling. If he is unknowingly an agent of death, he will also be the agent of his own death. The same, to be sure, is probably true for Sangrecco (why should he be spared?),[6] and the same is unquestionably true for the readers, who are complicit with death by reading about it, being thereby complicit with their own death in their understanding that that's what always lies at the end of the road of life.

Grampá's novel, his only one to date and one of the few Latin American graphic novels to be published in English translation,[7] deals very much in an existential cliché. But, then, graphic narrative is not a fertile field of philosophical speculation. Rather, the interest of *Mesmo Delivery* lies very much in the artistic value of the affective quality of its depiction of violence in a Brazilian industrial wasteland and, for the reader, the skillful utilization of the mystery surrounding the nature of the cargo the company is hired to haul. In this sense, Rufo, the has-been boxer, oblivious to the real nature of the job he has contracted for, is also something of an inverted Everyman icon for readers, who are equally oblivious to the mortal implications of the literary production they undertake to comprehend.

CHAPTER 7

The Unbearable Weight of Being:
Daniel Galera and Rafael Coutinho's *Cachalote*

In the evolution of contemporary graphic narrative, there is virtually a prevailing consensus to the effect that the graphic component (which means also the verbal one, since they are so inextricably combined) will lead the reader away from a satisfactory fulfillment of the desire for whatever might be called the realistic or conventional depiction of the texture of human society.[1] Much as creative photography and experimental film wish to defy the illusion of their power to depict lived human experience in a comfortably transparent fashion, graphic art (which, indeed, has a longer history as figural—in the sense of tropological—rather than figurative), as an intertwined component of narrative, aspires to a form of abstraction that promotes ambiguity and enhances a sense of mystery and wonderment.

I am not arguing that this sort of augmented realism—one interpretation of which is so-called magical realism—is an inherently constitutive part of contemporary graphic narrative. But it does tend to prevail, manifesting clearly the roots of these sustained narratives in the tradition of the weird, fantastic, edgy, and punk tradition of less structurally defined comic-book products, where there emerged a tradition of "violating" original criteria of noncontestational realism in favor of the outlandish, whether in the circumstantiality of phenomena like Rubber Man, the grotesqueries of Marvel Comics, or the speculative universes of the rich vein of science fiction in comic-book art.

It has been well established that one fundamental difference between comic-book art (with its rather ad hoc graphic exuberance and an accompanying thinness of narrative profundity) and graphic narrative as it has established itself as a contemporary cultural genre has been a set of underlying principles of narrative coherence that promote reader introspection and the sustained contemplation of a complex and ambiguous aesthetic object.[2] Over-the-top WHAM! BANG! KERPOW!, often tied to fanciful action images of raw physical experience, yield to the often highly nuanced and multiple ambiguous sequencing of lived human events, often with no conclusive sense of THE END.

Cachalote (2010), written by Daniel Galera (1979–) and drawn by Rafael Coutinho (1980–),[3] Brazilian artists with extensive artistic credentials, may be seen as an iconic representation of the frequently elliptical nature of Latin American graphic narrative. Five different narrative threads are developed in the three parts of this black-and-white novel, and it is important to underscore that they never intersect, although all are essentially anchored in contemporary São Paulo (one moves to Paris and other European locales), a city, as clichés would have it, highly propitious for the anomie of nonintersecting lives. The five threads are the following: (1) An over-the-hill Chinese action actor finds himself in São Paulo to promote his latest film. During this time a young man who is a member of the cast and, apparently, at least his aspirational lover, dies violently, the victim—maybe or maybe not—of foul play. (2) A bitter sculptor is obliged to face the emptiness of his life. (3) A spoiled playboy is exiled to Paris by his fed-up guardian uncle. (4) A hardware-store clerk's sexual fantasies lead him to a woman whose erotic will is stronger than his. (5) An apparently psychotic writer has a richer emotional relationship with his ex-wife than they had when they were married. Although the five threads are distributed in a nonproportional manner throughout the three parts of the novel and although they never intersect, not even to the point of the most happenstance presence of characters from one thread in another, they all come together under the aegis of the unbearable weight of human existence, as we see all five main characters (all five are men, evincing once again the androcentrism of the Latin American graphic narrative) struggling to survive existentially. Their existential struggle ranges from the grossness of the decadent Chinese actor to the excruciating Japanese erotic fantasies of the hardware-store clerk, from the loucheness of the playboy and the boorishness of the sculptor to the psychotropic drug-induced evanescence of the writer and his ex-wife, with whom he shares his medications.

However, there is a *cornice*, an enveloping narrative frame, for the five threads. I would maintain that that frame provides the overarching motivation for the five stories and their coherence within a single narrative project. The framework appears as a wordless sequence of six pages (nineteen panels) at the beginning of *Cachalote* and an equally wordless sequence of six pages (eighteen panels) as coda to the book. The image of the *cachalote* (cachalot = sperm whale) appears in both introit and coda and appears in the third version of the central narrative thread (i.e., the one that appears third in the initial sequence of the five), the one dealing with the bad-boy Rique. This frame and the dominant image of the sperm whale deserve elaboration, toward demonstrating how they key all five human stories being told.

In the introit, we see an older woman moving around her large mansion: she plays the piano, watches a romance story, and goes for a swim in her luxurious private pool. She is noticeably pregnant, while also notably aged, although no explanation is provided for this circumstance. The one additional frame in the introit, which disrupts the 18/18 distribution between introit and coda, is the image of a fetus floating in the amniotic fluid of the womb (by narrative juxtaposition, we suppose it is that of the pregnant older woman). When the woman, in the final half of the introit and after consulting her watch as though to determine it is time for this part of a daily routine, goes swimming, she and her fetus descend into the depths of the waters of the pool. As the woman surfaces, she comes face-to-face with a sperm whale, and she pats or strokes its snout. In a fashion characteristic of the noncontinuity between the five narrative threads, there is no formal marker of transition from one segment to the other, and we turn the page from this image to see a man urinating in a toilet, the only sign that we have left the introit and entered the story of the first of the five main characters—in this case, the wreck of a Chinese action-film star.

The coda appears at the end of the final sequence of the hardware-store clerk and his erotic companion, in which turning on the lights during intense lovemaking leads to the conceit of a black page that is blank except for the word "CLIC" and, in a circle in the center, as though an expanding point of light, the question (directed by the woman to the man), "Viu?" ([Get it?] no pag.).[4] Rather than seeing what the man is supposed to see or seeing the nature at this point of their complicated ritual lovemaking, we have the transition, on the next page, to the coda. The older woman sits on a beach chair with a closed book in her lap, watching her son, now about five years old, play on the beach. One of his five toys is a whale, which he is holding in his left hand; there are also a spaceman, a fishing boat, and a sea horse lying on the beach between his legs, and he holds a toy shark in his right hand. One is tempted to correlate these five toys with the five stories that have come between the introit and the coda. But, except for the fact that the whale appears in the final installment of Rique's story, there is no readily apparent symbology in the four other objects, although the reader, if he or she notices the presence of the five toys, might effect some sort of tenuous association. But then the boy looks up, stares at the roiling waves, and looks at the whale in his left hand. As though surprised, his mother looks up, squinting at the sea over the edge of her sunglasses. She folds the boy (we now see him naked) in a tight embrace and, as she lets him go, he walks out into the waves. The mother picks up the toys, folds her chair, and walks up the beach away from the waves.

This mysterious ending, which involves, we imagine, the disappearance of the boy into the waves—Has he seen a whale? *The* whale? Has he gone to search for it? Is the mother's apparent acceptance of the boy's disappearance into the waves as though it were an event foretold, related in some way to her experience in the introit with the whale in the backyard swimming pool? This would suggest a retroflexive reading grounded on a metaphor for the tenuousness of human life and the inevitability of our individual fall into nothingness. While the little boy is, as our cultural tropes would have it, as yet innocent of the complexities of life, he is also in a proleptic fashion an icon of each human being's disastrous and often deadly existence. Yet no matter how disastrous or deadly one's existence may be not only do we vanish into thin air, but much of the so-called living moments of our existence are equally the stuff of nothingness: when the writer's ex-wife, struck by deep anxiety as she waits with several other people at a bus stop, downs some of the psychotropic drugs he has just given her illegally, she literally disappears from the page, leaving a blank space between the waiting passengers on either side of her: the miracle of modern pharmaceuticals has not just anticipated her eventual existential vanishing, but they have afforded a dry run of that inevitability.

The boy's disappearance into the frothy waves of the ocean is the inverse of the appearance of the cachalot. The sperm whale, the cachalot, is characteristically one of a group of large whales that beach themselves, typically a couple of thousand a year; sometimes they are already dead, while sometimes they die as a consequence of the beaching, often from dehydration or because high tide covers over their blow hole and they drown.[5] There is considerable disagreement as to why this happens. But there is the fact that the group of whales that include the cachalot are among the few great mammals that dwarf human beings and leave them in awe. Also, they tend to belong to close-knit communities that make their separation from their fellow creatures highly suggestive of the way in which human beings can become alienated from the rest of their society, as is the case of several individuals in the Galera-Coutinho novel. Indeed, there is a double transition. First, it is the transition from the whale encountered by the pregnant woman in the introit to the man urinating in the toilet. But it is also the transition from the whale that mysteriously appears in her swimming pool to the "beached whale" (whether in general or in terms of his circumstantial appearance in Brazil) of the Chinese actor in decline, whose bloated body sprawls on his bed in very much a beached fashion. The prostitute who is with him must wonder where his rock-hard action figure body, which likely still prevails in his publicity shots, has gone.

Not only is there the abiding mystery of the beached whale, an image that goes back hundreds of years in artistic representations, but there is also the mystery of how and where it appears. Even if it is drawn ashore by prevailing tides, why is it that this whale has become beached and why is it in this particular location, with the possibility that the locations in which beached whales appear are unlikely sites, given the marine factors involved? To be sure, there are hardly abundant reports of whales appearing in domestic swimming pools, and besides, in the case of this whale it is not beached, even if it has scant chance of surviving the chlorinated and foodless waters of that body of water. A more conventionally beached whale is discovered by Rique, as he comes to the end of his rope on an abandoned beach outside Barcelona. At one point, there is some possibility that the animal may be a figment of his imagination, as it seems to have vanished. Rique, walking alone and, given the blanked-out look on his face, perhaps suffering from sunstroke, is also a likely candidate to disappear into thin air, at least in the sense of disappearing without a trace, severed from family, friends, and society at large, with none likely to take any note of his disappearance.

Clearly, the whale is important in framing the five narrative threads of *Cachalote* and in iconizing the irony of a presence that bulks large (human life in general, but the strong, reckless, and most careless lives of the five protagonists), only to disappear without a trace in a process of biological but, more importantly, psychological disintegration.[6] As such, it is a controlling magical icon that lends a heavy mystery to the existential commerce of these individuals and articulates a degree of unknowability that renders fevered human lives (from the louche to the exquisitely sensitive) utterly meaningless. If it is our convention to believe that the magical contains within it a human mystery we must strive to decipher in the best cabalistic fashion, there is little in narrative systems of the Galera-Coutinho narrative to make this possible. The proposition of a higher meaning to the existential events of human lives or to such mysterious signs as the key to an alternative reality is not forthcoming. That is, unless we can sustain the hypothesis that the tropological meaning of events is that they have no meaning.

The unbearable weight of human existence here is that it leads to the empty soundstage where the sculptor thought he has been collaborating in making a documentary on his life and work, to the abandoned beach where Rique can hardly strut his final stuff, to the darkened no-tell hotel room where the hardware-store clerk and his erotic partner (the masochist who, in the end, pushes the sadist beyond his limits) vanish into the dark produced by turning on the bedside lamp. Nothing times the magical still equals nothing, and what realism there is in the universe is neither deepened nor enhanced by the magical. In this fashion, the dense narrative texture of *Cachalote* is a correlative of the dense narrative texture of the universe we perceive: a lot of very heavy-duty things happen, but they leave nothing in their wake. The image of the mother just walking away from the beach after, apparently, her son has walked into the waves and sunk out of sight is certainly a very emphatic concluding one in which no amount of affective reader anguish, horror, or terror can alter the finality.

None of the foregoing is meant to signal that the dense narrative texture of *Cachalote* is not, in itself, narratively meaningful, only that there are no transcendent metaphysical implications to draw from it, aside from the metaphysical implication that there are no metaphysical implications. When viewed on the level of narrative structure, *Cachalote* is, indeed, a tightly structured semiotic edifice.

As I have noted, the narrative is explicitly divided into three parts, plus the introit and the coda, which are included in the first and third parts, respectively. These parts correspond to the internal narrative movements of classical Greek tragedy. I am speaking of the way in which the three parts of the narrative may be seen as a presentation or postulation of the characters and the situation of their lives. None is exemplary; rather, all seem to be quite screwed up, to put it bluntly, with the possible exception of the hardware-store clerk—and this depends on how one wants to read his involvement with the practice, highly dangerous and unquestionably sexist, of Japanese *kinbaku* (the ritual immobilization, via complex patterns of trussing with thick ropes, of women).[7] It is not a question of whether Vitório's sexual practices can, by any definition, be called consensual. Nor does it matter whether Lara's sexual fantasies are also his. It is an erotic spectrum that functions in tandem with that of the lives of the other four characters and, therefore, there is an implied symbiosis, an implied correspondence between their individual destinies, even if not all are as ruinous as, say, that of the loutish and decadent Chinese actor.[8] Thus, while it appears that we can only make a casual connection between the five main characters (one recalls that they never interact in the narrative), only the faintest coloration of them as somehow damned is forthcoming: they are, in the end, nothing more than a gallery of rather insignificant human beings, each insignificant in his own intimate way. That some may be immoral is only a further coloration beyond their basic parallels.

The second set of narrative developments corresponds to approximately what we can call the *peripeteia*, the reversal of fortune that will lead the main characters inevitably toward their individual forms of demise: the sculptor begins to perceive that the film in which he has agreed to star is going nowhere; the Chinese star appears to be kidnapped by individuals unknown; Rique buys a sports car and sets out on a highway to nowhere after having been rebuffed in every quarter in Paris; the wannabe writer's wife disappears into thin air after taking a handful of his psychotropics; Vitório discovers, at the hands of someone who appears to be her dark guardian angel, that he has gotten in over his head in his relationship with her. Perhaps none of these is as culminating an experience as tragic peripeteia, but Greek tragedy is not involved here. Suffice it to underscore how none of these "reversals" of fortune (perhaps the most momentous one might be in the case of Vitório, because of the intrinsic interest of frustrated sexuality and the deep terror we associate with the possibility of our entertaining erotic games going terribly wrong) augurs well for the personal story of each of the protagonists.

Each of the three sections is progressively shorter than the preceding one, and the third one, then, rushes, so to speak, toward the five individual denouements. This is the phase of anagnorisis, when the individual comes face-to-face with his own fate, which, in the case of the pathetic rather than tragic world of *Cachalote*, is the mess he has brought about. The second segment relating to the Chinese actor ends with someone from a group of young actors who befriends him asking "O que aconteceu no hotel, Xu?" ([What happened, Xu?] no pag.), the answer to which may or may not resolve the circumstances of the police warrant out for his arrest. One can envision a piteous reply that might provide an Aristotelian catharsis, while a reply that would confirm the police's suspicions would be more momentous. If a moment of anagnorisis is involved, in which the character must come face-to-face with his actions and the fate he has wrought through them, it is not shared with the reader. Anagnorisis becomes more of a narrative tease here, since one assumes the reader might well want to know what the nature of the relationship was between Xu and Jia, and how the latter fell to his death.

However, just as there is narrative fragmentation in the development of the three storylines, there is also, in the final section of *Cachalote*, narrative withdrawal and frustration, something like a *relatio interrupta* that correlates the unbearable weight of existence with the vacuousness at its core. One might entertain the proposition that each of the five protagonists here is, in one way or another, a beached whale, and perhaps Xu even more so given the bloated and decadent condition of his body. But, I would insist, the authors allow for only the most tenuous of associations, for to do otherwise would be to freight these individuals with an essentialist meaning that would be quite at odds with the discursive principles at play. Thus, the final segment for Xu involves the arrival of the police and his disappearance into a squad car. The woman who had asked him to explain what happened is left with an empty verbal gesture: "Pô" [Eh = who cares].

The sculptor decides to crash the soundstage with his automobile to find some trace of what has happened to the film crew that had convinced him to allow them to film his life. There is nothing there but a movie poster with the title *A face de mármore*; the police arrive; he is attempting to make a call to someone from the stationhouse; his wife picks him up; in the end, we see her studying the poster she takes from his hands after he falls asleep from exhaustion. We are left to wonder what it is he might have understood from the poster, although it would seem fairly clear that it is a less-than-generous reference to his hard-hearted ways that plays off of the stony nature of his visage and the marble with which a sculptor customarily works.

Fortunes appear to have changed for the better between the writer and his ex-wife, who although she confesses to him she is pregnant by her current lover, engages in a long and tender embrace with him. But there is no indication what this might mean, as the sequence concludes with their little girl, who has been told to go play with a puppy, follows the puppy to the edge of the park's iron fence, through which the puppy squeezes, only to be run over by a passing truck. What does little Bia understand from this event? The last we see of Rique is that he's stretched out on the beach, smoking a cigar, lying not quite in the shadow of the now very-much-present beached whale, whose immense size overshadows the insignificant Brazilian wannabe playboy.[9]

D. Galera and R. Coutinho, *Cachalote*

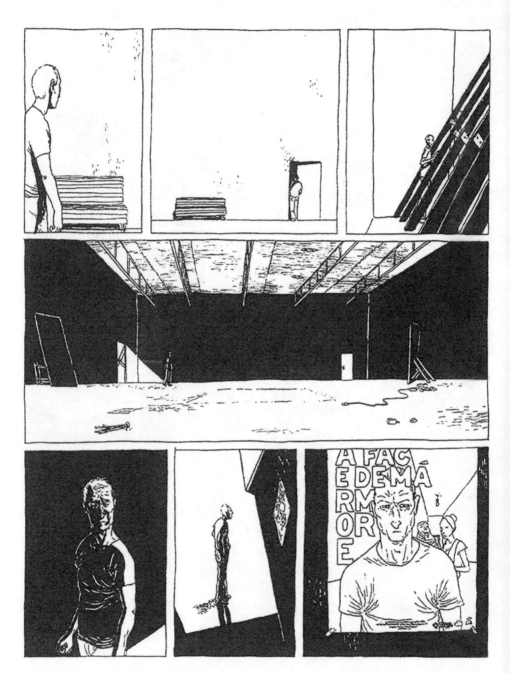

D. Galera and R. Coutinho, *Cachalote*

D. Galera and R. Coutinho, *Cachalote*

I have already characterized the concluding segment with Vitório and the now very demanding Lara. Suffice it to reinforce the conceit of the conclusion: she insists on their enacting their rituals of kinbaku with the lights on, but the blacked page, overlain by the CLIC of the lamp being turned on, makes it seem as though the sought-after illumination only produced the black hole of their passion, with the white dot containing the question "Viu?" as an ironic consequence of the failure of illumination.

In a sense, this concluding interrogative can be read as ironic for *Cachalote* as a whole: given the strategies of narrative displacement, what I am facetiously calling *relatio interrupta*, and a symbolism weighted with the nothingness of being, what can it be that the reader might or might not have seen? Now, if readers were following this commentary with the actual graphic narrative in hand, they would see that I, too, can be accused here of a certain amount of narrative displacement. The stories of the five protagonists are not just told three times, corresponding to the three divisions of the book. Rather, the third part of *Cachalote* in reality revisits each one of the five narrative threads twice, thereby drawing out the process of anagnorisis—and the concomitant suppression of an accompanying *catharsis.* The reader does not need a commentary to sketch out all of the details, but rather to give the sense of how each individual narrative thread is given final treatment. To be sure, the fact that the final "act" of the novel is a double *reprise* of each story only reinforces the overarching organizational principle of narrative displacement.

I want now to focus a bit more emphatically on the concept of narrative displacement. As has been widely recognized, such displacement, which Deleuze originally formulated with reference to film but which jibes fairly well with the pronounced cinematographic flow of the graphic narrative, is characteristic of the latter type of narrative. It is as though there were an imperative to move away from transparent narratives, both in the sense of motivation and meaning, but also in terms of cause-and-effect narrativity. To be sure, a classic Latin American work like Héctor Germán Oesterheld and Francisco Solano López's *El Eternauta* (1957–1959 in its original serial publication) does in fact—despite the conceit of a highly allegorical narrative within an enveloping proleptic frame that is grounded in the transcendent potential of art (see the discussion in the chapter on Oesterheld's narrative)—tell a very straightforward story of an alien invasion of Buenos Aires, its disastrous consequences, and the way in which a band of heroic men is able to save the day. Traditional or conventional cartoon art amply satisfies readerly demands (I am clearly evoking the legendary Barthian disjunction here between the readerly and the writerly) for narrative transparency, and it is the view of graphic fiction as edgy, vanguard, experimental that makes it reasonable, if not expected, that it will move toward the writerly end of the spectrum, toward complicating narrative paradigms and introducing audacious conjugations of narrative elements.

It is for this reason that one can find, as one variety of narrative displacement, an interest in certain modalities of the magical realism that equally characterized the innovative but strictly word-centered *nueva narrativa hispanoamericana* [new Spanish American narrative] of the 1960s and 1970s.[10] Although one may have little investment in a genre of magical realism in Latin American narrative, it is unquestionable that something like a magical-realist turn in Latin American writing occurred at one point as a rejection of the social-realist, documentary, quasi-sociological mode of so much early twentieth-century Latin American writing. Carlos Fuentes made this point very early in one of the first commentaries on the new Latin American novel. Where it has gone since has been of considerable controversy, and I am very much in agreement with my colleague Emil Volek as to what he calls *Macondismo*[11] and I would call the Macondo factor: the use of quirky, cute, charming, flamboyant, outrageous magical-fantastic elements in the service of a really quite disadvantageous, Third-Worldly belief in a primitive world more profoundly authentic than the dreary alienations of hegemonic Western capitalist "realities."

I affirm all of this here not to contribute anything significant to the debate, which may only serve to distract from text-centered analyses, but rather to situate Galera and Coutinho's work. Because when all is said and done, the narrative universe of *Cachalote* is hardly that of Gabriel García Márquez's Macondo, as in his *Cien años de soledad* (1967). Rather, it is very much postmodern, globalized São Paulo, Brazil. By the same token, *Cachalote* has little to recommend it as a screed on the spiritual depravations of late capitalism, although some may want to pick up on useful suggestions (e.g., the commercialism of the sculptor, the crazed-fan pursuit of the iconic international Chinese action star, Rique's playboy ways).

Where, then, do the elements one might wish to associate with magical realism go in *Cachalote*? Certainly, the process of narrative displacement is suggestive of an abstract narrative conjugation of the five story lines that is not in evidence on the level of *sujet*, the actual dynamics of narrative telling, since none of the five intersects with any of the others, except in the vague perception that all five are somehow beached whales of humanity. That this conjugation involves the mysterious cachalot that appears, may disappear, and may be there but unseen (the coda of the novel, involving the little boy's disappearance into the sea) is what propels this narrative beyond what could easily have been the depiction of the nitty-gritty texture of Paulistano daily life, with all its gallery of human possibilities synthesized in five protagonists. Indeed, as I have argued insistently here, the narrative tension of *Cachalote* rests on the interplay of a densely evoked quality of the mysterious (beginning with deep human emotions and motivations) and the otherworldliness of the iconic whale, especially in the guise in which it first appears, with the novel's deferral and, ultimately, denial of meaning. Such an affirmation is sustained by the way in which none of the five narrative threads is depicted in terms of any denouement whatsoever, no matter how much one keeps thumbing back in the various segments and despite the best efforts to review each thread on its own. The awe and circumstantially magical nature of these five urban Brazilian lives finally derives from the unbearable weight of unbeing and nonbeing.

CHAPTER 8

Copacabana and Other Hellish Fantasies:
Sandro Lobo and Odyr Bernardi's *Copacabana*

*Copacabana é mais do que um bairro. Ela é um limite entre a cidade
e o reduto. Copacabana trafega entre um sensível, visível externamente
e oferecido por formas, cores, arquitetura, tráfego e gente, e, por outro
lado, espaços reduzidos à invisibilidade da vida cotidana em que se
submergem milhares de pessoas, rostos anónimos carimbados por uma vida
desconhecida.*
*[Copacabana is more than just a neighborhood. It is the border between
the city and the stronghold. Copacabana deals in something palpable,
externally visible and eternally produced by forms, colors, architecture,
traffic, and people and, on the other hand, spaces reduced to the invisibility
of daily life in which thousands of people are swallowed up, anonymous
faces stamped by an unknown life.]*
COUTINHO 9

Rio de Janeiro's Copacabana beach and neighborhood is one of the
most privileged tourist fantasies of the world.[1] An image of Copacabana,
especially an aerial one featuring Sugar Loaf Mountain (Pão de Açu-
car) is sufficient to evoke Rio in its entirety, Brazil in its entirety, and the
most exciting and gorgeous tourist locales in their entirety. For over a
hundred years, Copacabana has been a symbol of the best of tropical va-
cationing, of the good life of brilliant scenery, beautiful people, excellent food, unending alcoholic consumption, easily available drugs, and
luscious sex. While the sex is hardly innocent—indeed, it is all the more
interesting because it is undoubtedly hard-edged, dangerous—the conjunction of sex and Copacabana symbolizes an erotic ideal that every
tourist is to believe is attainable in the magical realm of Copacabana.
And if the Brazilian Carnival is the apotheosis of unbridled sexuality, sex

and other accompanying pleasures enjoy their maximum fulfillment in the Carnival that plays out in Copacabana. Indeed, Copacabana is Carnival year-round. There is, in short, a deep well of mythification about life in Copacabana, whether experienced fleetingly as a tourist or lived on a daily basis in plenitude as the best Brazil has to offer itself and the world.

Hardly. Copacabana can, to be sure, be a richly rewarding experience if you know how to enjoy its many surfaces without having to invest in the cruel chimera of its sociological reality. One of the most densely populated places on Earth, Copacabana attracts the dregs of Brazilian and international society, hell-bent on eking out some measure of survival at the expense of the well-to-do who equate with a tropical paradise this short conch of seafront and barely a dozen blocks between it and the mountains that backdrop it. Rather it is a teeming mass of hustlers, prostitutes, murderous pimps, thieves, pickpockets, and con men—and the denizens of the fine hotels and elegant restaurants are only spiffier versions of the same. The vast underworld of Copacabana, which isn't quite so "under" because it is so massively apparent, is mostly from the interior, flocking to this golden strand to survive as best they can—or, perhaps better, as worst they can.

Sandro Lobo and Odyr's[2] *Copacabana* is a noirish evocation of the Copacabana underbelly,[3] but with the clever twist that the Gringo who at first seems to be a typical fall guy of con schemes continually being run against foreign visitors ends up prevailing over his aggressors.[4] There is something like a happy ending to the story, based on an interior narrative duplication in which a popular trash narrative models at least a fleeting moment of redemptive tenderness on the boardwalk (the famous Avenida Atlântica, consisting of mosaic tiles in a swirling geometric pattern of black and white). But neither of these denouements can occur without a considerable splash of blood, sexual abuse, and the efficacious exploitation of the weak and inattentive.

The most singular aspect of the Lobo–Odyr narrative is the decision to dispose completely with any pretense of touristic glamour. Known for its high percentage of days of sunshine and fairly even year-round temperatures, which lend themselves to shimmering color photography preferably in large formats, Copacabana is here represented not only in black and white, but with thick brushstrokes that are often so broad and heavy-handed that individual physical features are lost and the reader is at times hard put to grasp which character is being represented and, at times, whether that character is masculine or feminine. Moreover, backgrounds are shrouded in swaths and blocks of black, such that there can be no attempt to capture the play of sunlight that is reputed to be one of the most enduring charms of the beach and its environs. In fact, the first of fourteen chapters (the first thirteen numbered in Arabic numerals, the last unexplainedly as a roman number) takes place against the backdrop of a heavy rain in Copacabana, with the graphic representation of the raindrops making the panels even more obscure than in subsequent chapters. Nighttime scenes are equally more obscure, and the alternation of line-drawn scenes versus black-shadow representation, even when the action is not ostensibly taking place in a darkened room or in the unlighted night, makes black all the more predominant.

Copacabana is really two narratives plus, only partially, the inserted narrative of a trashy romance novel. It is first and foremost a detailed sketch of prostitutes and the men who exploit them (clients, pimps, and other participants in the infrastructure of prostitution). About a half-dozen women who work the streets, bars, hotels are portrayed in terms of the microsociety they constitute. They come and go in shared living quarters (often in rundown boardinghouses or fleabag hotels), sometimes lucky enough to share, if only temporarily, more decent quarters. They interact, sometimes in ruthless competitiveness, sometimes in sisterly solidarity, in the bars and other locales where they are likely to find their clients. And they are routinely equalized in the brutalizing treatment they receive at the hands of both their pimps and their clients, as much physically as psychologically. While exploitation by the police is not represented in these chapters, there is another form of exploitation that does not routinely get covered in the customary representations of the lives of prostitutes. One of them, Diana, who is, typically, from the so-called interior (that is, anywhere outside of the large Brazilian cities located either directly on the Atlantic or close to it), pretends to her mother, who calls her frequently, that she works the nightshift in a hospital. Her mother seems to know full well that this is not true, as she calls her daughter to demand insistently that she send her large sums of money, much more than she could reasonably make in a presumably decent occupation. Diana, who always treats her mother with respect, redoubles her trade on the streets, fearful that the charade will be disrupted; Diana's mother also insistently (in a gesture of psychological cruelty?) inquires if any of the doctors at the hospital have shown an interest in her.

There is, however, a central crime story to *Copacabana* that does not fully emerge until chapter 5. It involves a Gringo (probably a North

S. Lobo and B. Odyr, *Copacabana*

American, since his Portuguese is peppered with American slang and colloquialisms) who has already been introduced, someone who typically partakes in the fleshly delights of the beach and has large sums of money to throw around. Prompted by their shared pimp, Diana and Suelen (= Sue Ellen: both are noms de guerre, of course) engage in a setup of the Gringo, who is interested in having sex with the two of them together. Diana is directly drawn into the scheme by Suelen, whose idea is to spike the Gringo's drink and then they will make off with the money he has stashed somewhere in his hotel room. The plan backfires, as the Gringo presses his drink on Diana, who passes out. Suelen then bashes the Gringo with the bottle and makes off with the money. Somewhat unrealistically, she is able to get the pimp to spirit the unconscious Diana out of the hotel and back to the apartment the two women share, where she hides the money she has been carrying since finding it in the hotel room, telling the pimp that she hadn't been able to find anything. Eventually Suelen will be murdered, and Diana experiences a series of assaults in order to wrest from her the money then in her possession. In due course we find out that the Gringo has hired a detective to find the money. He finally catches up with Diana on his own (after the detective and his associate are killed in a narrative excursus that involves a retired army general whose cane has a hidden and lethal dagger). One might have expected him to kill her as part of the recovery of his money, but he only ties her up to a bed, where she is found by the woman whose apartment Diana and Suelen had been housesitting temporarily.

All of this has a happy ending of sorts when Diana discovers that an author of trashy romance narratives, who ends up in the middle of the fray when the retired army general saves the day with his dagger cane, is someone she really likes, and the novel closes with them walking hand in hand on the Avenida Atlântica that borders the beach. In the novel she reads by this author, a beautiful taxi boy and a millionaire who seems to have acquired her wealth in dubious ways fall thunderously in love, to live happily ever after in the Copacabana tropical paradise. Diana (and the author) may understand profoundly that this is all so much silly fantasy. Yet after their harrowing escapades with the failed con scheme that Diana was unwittingly drawn into, holding hands (the one act of love they say they have not experienced together in Copacabana) has at least a momentarily redemptive quality against the backdrop of so much ugliness.

One need not speculate on the conventionalized cop-out of the hand-holding idyll suggested by Diana and Morcego's final scene, except to say that, in addition to mitigating the ugliness of the majority of the narrative representations in *Copacabana*, it does have a certain unexpected humor to it: they have made love in so many different ways up and down the strand that merely holding hands is a tender threshold experience for them, especially since it is clear that Diana will consider continuing to make her living in prostitution. So maybe the ending is not so conventionally happy after all, but nicely ironic: nothing changes, but there are moments when the struggle for survival in Copacabana is not totally hellish in the end.

Lobo and Odyr's story, however, leaves little doubt that theirs is pretty much a strident alternative story of life in the fabled beach area. Their narrative makes use of a number of visual and narrative tropes that have the effect of emphasizing their specific interpretations. For example, since there is a particular emphasis on Copacabana as a site of prostitution (certainly a sociologically determinable fact), narrative connections are made such that the entire world of Copacabana portrayed (bars and restaurants; streets and, of course, the beach itself; living spaces; commercial enterprises; entertainment venues) and its characters (the prostitutes themselves; their clients; tourists in general; employees of the infrastructure of tourism, including especially hotel employees, barmen, waiters, and cab drivers; drug dealers; even Diana's gynecologist) are engaged in maximizing prostitution in direct and indirect ways, in literal and metaphorical terms.

One of the curious visual elements in the novel is not just the reliance on phones, but conventional phones. It is unusual for a strip published in 2009 to have virtually no reference to cell phones,[5] although most certainly prostitutes in Brazil today, a country that is typically in the vanguard of technological innovation, communicate with clients and pimps and each other via cell phone. Yet, in addition to domestic and commercial establishments' fixed landline phones, the strip makes recurring visual reference to one of the icons of Brazilian public space since around 1973, the *orelhão* (literally, big ear). The *orelhão* is the public phone with a Plexiglas enclosure, painted blue, orange, or yellowish orange. It allows for the user's head to be isolated from street noises while speaking on the phone. Now mostly gone or in disrepair, the *orelhão* was once a symbol of the modernization of the Brazilian communications network after the 1964 military coup and its promise of prosperity. However, with the rise of cell phones in Brazil (urban Brazil, at least, probably has the highest per capita cell phones in Latin America), the *orelhão* no longer serves a major function, and many of the phones are now eyesores, festooned with graffiti and dangling receivers or a gaping interior where the phone has been ripped out.

However, for Lobo–Odyr, the modernistically designed phone booth is a symbol of Copacabana and, as a medium of communication, it is an icon of the exploitation of the vast enterprise of prostitution. And if Diana's mother's excessive petitions for monetary remittances from her daughter are part of her understanding that her daughter is engaged in prostitution and not employed at a rate of far less income in a hospital, we see her communicating with her mother via such a public phone booth. This, in turn, underscores Diana's character as a dutiful daughter who feels she must remain in respectful contact with her mother from the metropolis where she has gone to work, since the public phone only allows for her to call her mother and not for her mother to call her. That is, Diana has internalized her exploitation by her mother, since it is she who calls home, essentially putting herself in a position to have demands made on her income. At another point in the story, her mother does call Diana on the phone where she is housesitting, but it is Diana who leaves the lines of communication open, even if she is always in a hurry to hang up because she is late for work. In addition to arranging assignations, conventional phones are used in the story to set up con games, to track the whereabouts of the participants in them, to make deals, to harass, and to engage in forms of extortion. For this reason, equally anachronistic (perhaps better, almost but not totally) are phones with answering machines, which allow for the storage and playback of the messages of the aforementioned forms of criminal commerce.

Phones in *Copacabana*, therefore, exercise an important metonymic function, tying various segments of the narrative together on the basis of the way in which they signal illicit or marginally illicit activities.[6] Graphic representation (for example, film, television, and photography, in addition to graphic novels and their predecessors—and, now, cousins once removed—the comics) relies heavily on the use of icons, especially metonyms, for holding a story together in the brief space assigned for its development. While characters whose physical traits and dress may exercise this function (Diana always appears in public in what we conventionally recognize as the raiment of whores—itself metonymic in nature, such as the fishnet stockings or the ultra-miniskirt and plunging neckline), and locales recur (for example, the bar where Diana mostly solicits her customers or the hotel where she takes them), circumstantial icons are important for linking segments of the action together, which here means the way in which phones are involved in the unsuccessful robbery of the Gringo and its deadly aftermath or the way in which the phone link between Diana and her mother speaks implicitly to the biographical trajectory of young women from the impoverished outback of the mother she leaves behind to the scenic strand of prostitution and its violence that Copacabana embodies.

Another such metonymic device in the novel is the penis. Of course, one would expect the anatomical aspects of sex to be present in a novel dealing with prostitution. And rather than the possibilities by which high-class prostitution may involve a broad range of physical activities that may or may not end up with the money shot involving the genitals, the sort of quickie trade Diana engages in is necessarily the most rapid dispatch possible of the money shot.[7] Fellatio fulfills this requirement nicely, and the so-called *microfone* is the least expensive of the sex acts because it is the quickest. Vaginal sex may require longer and anal sex, while it may be preferred to avoid the possibility of pregnancy, involves other potential problems. As a consequence, time and again, the penis is displayed as part of the quicker oral sex act.[8] By contrast, evocation of anal sex is part of the discourse of clichés of rough sex as a paradigm as much for prostitution, real sexual fulfillment, and sex as a form of physical abuse.[9] What is particularly noteworthy here is the way in which *Copacabana*, no matter what sexual scenario is being represented, makes it clear that condoms are never used.[10] If the penis is present as an explicit metonym for the sort of prostitution exemplified by the streets of the Copacabana district, the absence of the condom in its representation is, to extend a concept from linguistic analysis, a zero metonym (i.e., something whose absence is meaningful) for its violent nature. The refusal to use a condom, especially during promiscuous sex, is allegedly the imposed decision of the client, but it is important to note that when Diana refers to the pricing of her services, she does not make a fee distinction based on whether a condom is utilized (15).

Equally metonymic is the Gringo, both in his ostentatious display of his money and in how he is, thus, presented as standing in for the foreigners who are such easy marks in the haunts along the beach. It would be a typical gesture of cultural nationalism to portray the foreigner, especially the American, in such a way, but it is noteworthy that, although the Gringo cannot figure out in advance that he is being set up as he moves to fulfill his desire to have sex with two prostitutes at the same time, he is able to track them down and recover his money. This he

S. Lobo and B. Odyr, *Copacabana*

does by hiring a local detective, who has no qualms about pursuing the two women, killing Suelen, busting up Diana's place, and then returning with an associate who is willing to rape her boyfriend to force her to say where the money is (it is in a shopping bag she "accidentally" leaves behind at her gynecologist's office).

When the detective and his associate are killed by the retired general, the Gringo, who now knows she has the money, closes in on her, but only ties her up to give him time to vanish with his dollars. Rather quaintly, then, *Copacabana* shows the Brazilians to be murderous in their pursuit of Suelen and Diana, but the actual victim, the Gringo, is shown almost to be benevolent: he doesn't even beat Diana up or rape her in the process of recovering what she has stolen from him. One supposes this is a narrative correlative to the way in which it was really Suelen and not Diana who engaged in violence against the Gringo and made off with his money, leaving Diana to spend two days sleeping off the knockout drug and the Gringo with his head bashed in from the bottle Suelen wields when she realizes that he has (innocently? generously? as a precaution?) given his drink to Diana rather than taking it himself. This inversion of the cultural stereotype whereby the disaffected foreigner exercises retaliatory violence against the locals who have swindled him ties in with the trashy romance story Diana is reading and the way in which she and the author of that romance (who has been saved from anal rape) walk off down the Avenida Atlântica hand in hand.

The mitigation in such a fashion of the essentially unrelieved violence of Diana's world as presented in *Copacabana* may be a form of cruel optimism (i.e., it won't take long for the norm of noirish and unstinting violence to reassert itself), and it may trade shamelessly on the motif of the prostitute with a heart of gold (Diana is really an innocent, as underscored by the respectful way in which she allows her mother to manipulate her). But, then, the myths and fantasies regarding Copacabana, as commercial and hokey as they may often be, deserve some measure of investment. After all, in the closing scene of Roman Polanski's *Chinatown* (1974), when all the corruption and mayhem lie nakedly exposed and Jack Nicholson's Jake Gittes is cautioned "Forget it, Jake, it's only Chinatown," it does nothing to diminish the tourist allure of one of America's most favored ethnic neighborhoods.[11] Such must be the case with Copacabana: as hellishly as it has treated Diana, the undulating mosaic of the boardwalk she treads hand in hand with Morcego must still mean something romantic—no matter how precariously.

CHAPTER 9

Days of Death: Fábio Moon and Gabriel Bá's *Daytripper* as Existential Journey

When the Livraria Cultura, at the shopping center known as the Conjunto Nacional on the Avenida Paulista in the financial district of São Paulo, opened in 2012 its fifth locale in the Conjunto—Geek, Etc.—it constituted an important confirmation of the symbolic and commercial status of alternative, cutting-edge, and marginal forms of popular culture. One of those forms, occupying a good share of the second floor of Geek, is the graphic narrative. The graphic narrative section had been among the most visited of the main outlet of Cultura in the Conjunto and its other branches.

Although the section may receive less general public attention than it previously did (the whole aura of Geek is not conducive for patronage by the staid), it is at least now framed, rather than as a caboose of conventional print narrative, as part of a cultural vanguard. Viewed in whatever commercial and advertising context, the most casual perusal of the material carried under the rubric of graphic narrative reveals that the bulk of it, whatever its thematic and artistic codes may be, involves titles translated into Portuguese, paradigmatically from English (Japanese manga, one seems to remember, has its own section). While there is a fair range of original Brazilian material, the fact that the preponderance of material is translated from other languages in reality carries out the scheme of the main store of Cultura, where there is a relatively small (and often unkempt) section of Brazilian literature alongside a far more extensive representation of sections of foreign literature in original languages and in translation into Portuguese. Since one assumes that Cultura caters to the tastes of its clients, clearly the demand for original Brazilian literature, conventional print or graphic, is in the minority.

It would be difficult to find any conventional Brazilian novelist writing directly in English, even if Jorge Amado and Paulo Coelho may or may often seem to sell more in English translation than in their original Portuguese. However, one of the most fascinating phenomena of Brazilian graphic narrative is, in fact, a Brazilian set of twins, Fábio Moon and Gabriel Bá (born in 1976) who, after enormous success since ca. 2000 with their narratives in Portuguese, turned in 2007 to working directly in English. *De:Tales: Stories from Urban Brazil* (2006) was nominated for the Will Eisner award in 2008, and their second collaborative work in English, *Daytripper* (2010), won the Eisner award in 2011 in the category of Best Limited Series. I will have more to say later about this strategic linguistic decision, but, on the face of it, it has very much to do with the rise of the graphic novel as a major cultural genre in English and with the fact that, in Brazil, there is an association of the cultural vanguard with the English language, as well as a vast reservoir of native speakers of Brazilian Portuguese who are fluent in English and are directly conversant with culture in English, especially American culture. This does not extend, perhaps, to the typical customer of Geek, Etc. (although *Daytripper*, published by trendsetting DC Comics of New York, was available on the shelf at the time of a visit to the store in early July 2013), but it does index a very important dimension of cultural dynamics today in, at least, the cultural capital that is São Paulo.

I have written elsewhere about the importance of the work Moon and Bá have done in conjunction with each other, as well as with other artists (not unsurprisingly, in the case of the latter instances, exclusively in English), and one of the ten chapters of my book on São Paulo and cultural production is devoted to the ingenious short stories that make up *De:Tales.* Here is how their work is framed in that study:

All three [of Moon's and Bá's principal volumes in Portuguese: *O gira-sol e a lua* ([The sunflower and the moon] 2000), *Meu coração, não sei porque* ([My heart, I know not why] 2001), and *Mesa para dois* ([Table for two] 2006)] are of considerable artistic value and contain original conceptions—if not in narrative language, in graphic representation—that include complex juxtapositions of circumstances and events. Of particular interest are lengthy dialogues broken up into chained balloons that crisscross each other and create the illusion of rapid interchanges by exchanging the position of the two characters' textual balloons: A's is above B's head, and vice versa, with the balloon's tail indicating which enunciation belongs to which character. (Foster, *Sao Paulo* 139)

Daytripper first appeared in a ten-issue limited series between February and November 2010 with Vertigo Comics, a division of DC Comics that published the single-volume compilation in 2010.[1]

Daytripper is one of the most ingenious graphic narratives I have read. Where many graphic novels come off as little more than technically more proficient forms of Marvel Comics and the like—this is essentially one way to react to Alan Moore's overrated *Watchmen* series (1987, etc.)— the Moon-Bá collaboration has a quality to it that provides for a unique cultural product. While the listing of the names suggests that Fábio Moon is responsible for the narrative and Gabriel Bá for the illustrations (Dave Stewart is credited with the coloring and Sean Konot with the lettering), collaboration is so close, so symbiotic between the two of them that this is a unified product with shared and exchanged responsibilities. The graphic artistry of *Daytripper* is impressive, with effective rhetorical use of colored and monochromatic frames and a cinematographic quality to the perspective, with an array of close-ups, pans, zooms, reverse shots, and frames of varying dimensions and juxtapositions.

But what is most impressive about *Daytripper* is the sheer originality of the narrative conception. *Daytripper* tells, in no particular chronological order (except that the last of the ten chapters does focus on old age; chapter 5 focuses on the main character as a little boy), ten instances in the life of Brás de Oliva Domingos, an aspiring novelist who works early in his life writing obituaries for a São Paulo newspaper. Eventually married and with a young son, Brás is successful as a novelist and is able to transition to full-time creative writing. Throughout his career, he has a complicated relationship with his artistic mother and with his father, who is a famous novelist, such that there is very much an Oedipal relationship between the two men. The ten narratives are interconnected in many clever ways, causing the reader to entertain the proposition of associative thought, as opposed to the unilinear logic of so-called realistic storytelling. Moreover, while there is a specific narrative arc for each one of the ten chapters, there are in any one chapter flashbacks and foreshadowings of the plotline of the other nine. The result is a narrative complexity very much at odds with the simplistic succession of events in comic books and in even the still predominately jejune modes of storytelling in less thoughtfully executed forms of graphic narrative.

What makes *Daytripper* particularly interesting is the topic of death. Although other instances of death occur in the story, the chapters are framed, at least until Brás gets his own literary career off the ground, by his occupation as an obituary writer. Obituaries are, to be sure, biographical vignettes and, when written by editorial personnel (as opposed to by some interested relative or friend of the deceased, in which case, while they may undergo some editing by newspaper staff for inappropriate details, they essentially appear as written), obituaries correspond to the ideological parameters of the newspaper that undertakes to publish them; obviously, not everyone who dies merits an obituary, and not all of the details of someone's life are pertinent to the note. In this sense, Brás, as the author of death notices, participates in a highly charged field of information surrounding the death of someone whose demise is of sociohistorical importance.

By contrast, all ten of the freestanding chapters of *Daytripper* end with Brás's own death, usually in a surprising, accidental, and violent fashion in circumstances beyond his control. Only at the end of the last chapter does Brás give himself over to suicide, by drowning as part of an affirmation of the meaningful nature of this, his "final" death. Certainly, Brás cannot have died ten times—not, at least, in any real-world universe. And yet these are not metaphorical deaths: their generally violent and unexpected nature gives them material finality. But they occur here in an interlocking—or rhizomic—fashion that, while not metaphors, constitutes verisimilar indexes of the lived quality of life and its mortal inflections.

If we reduce these inflections to an inventory, they sound like meager clichés: all life is a progression toward death; we are dying from the moment we are born; death defines conclusively the nature of one's life; death is the most unimpeachable evidence of our cosmic helplessness; death as much as life defines our relationship to others; all culture is ultimately about death. It is noteworthy that, while so much Brazilian culture is eschatological, with the religious belief in a life beyond death, the Moon-Bá universe is not, and, hence, death represents an undeniable finality of human destiny.

None of the chapters of *Daytripper* is driven by a sense of death or of the need to prepare for it, although at the end of chapter eight, Brás dies of complications during surgery to remove a brain tumor while on a book tour, and at the end of chapter ten he commits suicide. But in the case of the former, the narrative focuses on his family and not on his preparation for surgery, with the inevitable knowledge of the risks involved. In the case of the last chapter, we only know for certain he is going to commit suicide when he begins to walk out into the water, and we do not actually see him drowning. Thus, the moment of death, as unquestionably significant as it is, is virtually a closing narrative point of punctuation and not the business of the narrative in any one of the chapters.

So, then, what is the narrative substance of the chapters? Quite simply, the dense texture of lived human experience: one's relationship with one's parents, with one's partners and friends, with the meaningful contexts and situations of life, and, as one might expect, with the dreams and illusions that motivate one's life. This is also all pretty clichéd when enumerated in this fashion, and it is even more so when one understands that *Daytripper* essentially takes place in São Paulo, where the texture of daily life is hardly amenable to taking life easy. This is quite evident in the stories in *De:Tales*. While there are some moments of urban turmoil (and, indeed, some instances of Brás's death are provoked by urban violence, such as his being gunned down in a bar holdup in one, or getting run down crossing the street by a delivery truck in chapter 3, or being part of a chain reaction of colliding big rigs on a peripherally urban national freeway [chapter 6]). But where the earlier *De:Tales* is all about hostile urban textures (specifically in São Paulo), *Daytripper* is in general remarkably benign about big-city day-to-day living, which, one could assert, only serves to put into greater relief that moment of violent death when it arrives.

One of the most interesting chapters is that devoted to Brás's friend Jorge, whom he originally met at the university (Universidade de São Paulo, one assumes). Brás is quintessentially European in appearance, and he looks rather like Fábio Moon himself, although mostly the two nonidentical twins appear together, with little in the way of indicators as to who is who, part of the profound symbiotic nature of their work together. Jorge, by contrast, is quintessential Afro-Brazilian. Both men are tall, but Jorge is thinner, and his wild hair (often portrayed with dreadlocks) contrasts with Brás's more conventionally middle-class look. Jorge is a photographer, and a deep friendship develops between them. Early in the narrative (chapter 2), they travel together to Salvador, where Jorge introduces Brás to the sexual delights of the Bahian capital, playing enabler to his romantic involvement with a stunningly beautiful *mulata*, with whom Brás eventually lives for seven years in São Paulo before their affair turns sour.

Jorge reappears in a dramatic fashion in chapter 7. At one point, he drops out of urban life, and we eventually learn that he has holed up in the remote beach village of Acemira. During Jorge's absence of about a half-dozen years, Brás has never forgotten about him, and the chapter is built as much around Brás's final success as a novelist as it is around his tender memory of his vanished friend: superficial fame versus a life-defining friendship. His last contact with Jorge came as a call from a public phone, and the communication was cut short when the time ran out on Jorge's phone card. Now Brás receives a postcard from Jorge from Acemira with the terse message "I can't do it without you. J." The connection between the two narrative sequences is Brás's realization that literary success has given him a host of illusory friends who bask in his fleeting public fame, which only provokes his return to the profound memories of what he has shared with Jorge as the one true friend of his life. The narrative sequencing is very well handled here, and it is intersected by Brás's wife's impatience with his melancholy when the postcard from Jorge arrives. Clearly, Brás is brought suddenly face-to-face with the unresolved pain of Jorge's disappearance, while at the same time his wife perceives very clearly the threat that such melancholy represents for their relationship.

It is here that the narrative's confirmation of the depth of homosocial attachment between the two men collides with the presumed primacy of his heterosexual commitments to his wife and son. It is not that the two are incompatible in and of themselves. In an abstract fashion and in everyday practice homosociality is the basis of solidarity and communication—and the exchange of masculine power—between male social subjects in the sort of a masculinist world that still predominates in Brazil. But specific homosocial bonds may be perceived to be a threat to heterosociality (especially the bourgeois family), particularly when there is the concomitant perception that the homosocial has the potential to veer off into the homoaffective. It is not so much that *Daytripper* comes to insinuate a homoaffective relationship between the two men, whose friendship, significantly, predates Brás's marriage and family. Yet there is a realm of problematical relationship between the two men that may have something to do with Jorge's disappearance, the enigmatic meaning of the terse sentence on his postcard, and the extent of Brás's melancholy such that, despite his wife's resistance, makes him dash off in search of Jorge.

What Brás finds does nothing to resolve whatever his psychological turmoil may be. Jorge has ended up in the remote (fictional) fishing village of Acemira. After exhausting his resources, and his welcome beyond his resources, at the local hotel, he has been kicked out and has taken refuge first in a partially constructed building and then in a dirty hut on the beach. When Brás reaches Acemira and the hotel, the owner's daughter tells him that, with his energy and wit, he had become a

F. Moon and G. Bá, *Daytripper*

welcome addition to the town, and that he spent a great amount of time writing postcards. When her father finally kicked him out for nonpayment, she found the one postcard left behind and since it had an address on it, she put it in the mail. Now that Brás has shown up, she leads him to the beach and points out the hut. When he asks how she knew who he was, she produces a torn part of the cover of his best-selling novel.

As Brás approaches the hut, the coloring of the narrative changes from rich daylight colors to a twilight orange and purple, tinged with black—literally, the color of a bad bruise. When Brás enters the hut, he finds Jorge lounging on the sand in squalor, surrounded by a blanket of unmailed postcards. Brás attempts to reason with Jorge, but Jorge says it is all too late for that. As the coloring shifts almost exclusively to the shades of a bruise, Jorge pulls out a long knife with a needle-point tip. Over Brás's protestations, Jorge, saying "I'm sorry I left. I wasn't a good friend" (173), slashes his wrist, and his blood spurts against a totally black background. When Brás rushes forth to stop Jorge from further self-mutilation, Jorge calmly says "'Now hold still'" (173, in quotation marks as though he were quoting a doctor), and proceeds to plunge the knife into Brás's body: "'This will only take a minute'" (174) as he continues to quote from something from memory.

Briefly, the sequence of Brás's murder is interrupted by three panels that return to the daylight, a flashback to the time at which they posed for a final picture together before undertaking the return from the trip to northern Brazil they had taken together years before (and which is related in chapter 2). As the sequence of Brás's murder resumes, Jorge mounts the supine Brás and stabs him repeatedly; he then falls on his back and stabs himself in the chest. This sequence, although without a change in coloring, also continues a flashback to their youthful time together, and Jorge's citation of their words from that time spills over into the main sequence. Thus, the narrative seeks to achieve a correlation between the present moment of murder-suicide and an earlier time of deep personal communication between the two men, between the sense that it is too late and something has been lost and a moment of euphoric communion: "BRÁS: You've got all the answers, huh? JORGE: Only for the good questions" (175).

What is it that Jorge feels has been lost between the two of them, beyond perhaps the cliché that time destroys all youthful illusions? All of the chapters end with a final panel in which the narrator relays, in an obituary-like fashion, the circumstances of Brás's death in that chapter. In the case of this chapter, the obituary is unusually long, and it

F. Moon and G. Bá, *Daytripper*

ends with the statement, in the sort of clipped tone of well-written obituaries, "He was thirty-eight and he died because he believed in friendship" (176).

Daytripper is not Jorge's story, so we never get a formal obituary for him. But what might the narrator have given as the reason for Jorge's death at this point? He seems as if he believed in friendship, or in something that kept him emotionally tied to Brás and impelled him to spend his days writing postcards to his now successful novelist friend. What was it he could not do without Brás? The fact that all of this is left in suspense enhances the sinister quality of this chapter in the end, with his garish coloring, which continues in the final "obituary" panel, with the image of the two bloodstained bodies lying on the beach, with Brás's tote-bag and Jorge's unsent postcards strewn around the foreground.

It would be stressing the obvious to belabor the so-called Freudian nature of Jorge mounting Brás and proceeding to penetrate him repeatedly with the knife. But clearly there is a deep undercurrent of affective attachment between the two men that turns into fatal violence, an affective attachment that both leads Brás to seek Jorge out after so many years of absence and Jorge to have fetishized their relationship in terms of the piles of unsent postcards. Whether this attachment is homoerotic on one or another of their parts; whether Jorge is ultimately driven by a sense of loss when Brás marries a woman, a sense of loss that evolves into jealous rage (despite the fact that, in chapter two, we see Jorge as an enabler of Brás's relationship with a woman); whether the murder-suicide is the only corporal climax left to Jorge as an option; and whether what Jorge cannot do alone is live without Brás's physical proximity: these are questions the strip leaves unanswered and, as far as the text literally says, may not even be questions the narrator is disposed to entertain.

After all of the random violence Brás has witnessed and experienced, the series of which leads repeatedly to his iconic death at recurring high points of his existential passage through the world—his "daytripping," as though they were nothing more than a series of agreeable parentheses in his humdrum routine—the fact is that this is the most dreadful and the most painful violence he experiences and is the one that is the most profoundly undecipherable in the juxtaposition between the nobility of the friendship between Brás and Jorge, which drives the former to seek out his old friend in the desire to address the latter's apparent deep suffering and the fatally sinister nature of that suffering. Unrequited homoerotic suffering is in itself not sinister, if that is, indeed, what is involved here. Nor is any other kind of suffering to which Jorge may be subject

F. Moon and G. Bá, *Daytripper*

that he at some point feels Brás can help him with. What is sinister is the turn that suffering takes, both in Jorge's self-immolation in his reclusion in the dirty hut on the beach of Acemira and in his brutal murdering of his "lost" friend. Stewart's coloring of the strip is masterful here, and in the way in which so much of this one central chapter is so unique from the others, it is the only one in which the semiotics of color constitute such a radical shift from the first to the last panels that make it up.

All of Brás's deaths are eloquently iconic in the context of the chapter-by-chapter narrative circumstances of his life: being shot as part of a random holdup, dying in a plane crash, being the victim of a traffic pile-up on the freeway, not making it through brain surgery, being accidentally electrocuted in an attempt to rescue a fallen kite (the names of each of the chapters are numbers that express the age of Brás when death comes to him). But there is so much that is particularly resonant about chapter 7—the friendship with Jorge, the complex relationship with his wife, his love for their son, the memory of the trip with Jorge to northern Brazil when they were young men, his success as a novelist, the consolidation of his place as a social subject that is proportionally inverse to Jorge's decline, and the horrible possibility that that consolidation may be, in fact, what destroys Jorge—that it is very much the narrative center of the novel.

With *Daytripper*, Fábio Moon and Gabriel Bá demonstrate not only that they are capable of uniquely original narratives, but that the overall quality of this title makes it an important entry in the bibliography of contemporary Brazilian fiction and a fine example of the level of the graphic narrative attained in Brazilian culture. Both artists have recently worked on projects that, if only momentarily, dissolve their long partnership, especially Bá, who has done illustrations for several US-based series.[2] Yet, *Daytripper* has so much originality to it that one cannot believe that it will not soon be followed, as was the equally unique *De:Tales*, by further collaborative work.

A few observations about the use of English in *Daytripper* are in order by way of conclusion. One understands the deep wellspring of Brazilian cultural nationalism associated with the question of language. Brazilian Portuguese stands in a complexly geometric relationship to Peninsular Portuguese, to surrounding dialects of Latin American Spanish, to indigenous languages, to immigrant languages within Brazil (Yiddish, German, Italian, and Japanese are notable here), and to prestige international models: formerly French and now English, especially American English. One also takes note of bilingual projects involving Spanish and Portuguese, *portuñol,* which a novelist of the stature of Wilson Bueno has entertained. The fact that *Daytripper* was written in English (presumably directly by one or both of the brothers, since there is no acknowledgment of any translation; the English is very good, and only one example of a nonnative construction is readily apparent) has, one speculates, nothing to do with Moon and Bá seeking entry into the geometric multilingualism that is part of Brazilian cultural history and everything to do with market opportunism. The graphic novel is unquestionably an Anglo-American phenomenon, despite excellent non-English examples and the Spanish and Portuguese examples that are part of my current research.

Graphic narratives, with few exceptions, appeal to a mass-market audience, and only an extremely limited number, like Art Spiegelman's *Maus* (1991) can aspire to translation into other languages. Brazil is, to be sure, an immense market, and Cultura's Geek, Etc. division is a good commercial response to its potential. Yet judging by the material on the shelves at Geek, the anticipated audience is for foreign material and for material that is formulaic and sensationalist in a way that *Daytripper* is not. *Daytripper,* according to listings in OCLC WorldCat, has been translated into French, Danish, Spanish, Italian, and Portuguese. Whether *Daytripper* and Moon's and Bá's other work in English might end up being considered Brazilian literature by bibliographers and critics remains to be seen. But overlooking this eminently Brazilian cultural product because it was originally published in English is to ignore some of the best work being done by graphic fiction artists in Brazil or anywhere else in the world.

Women's Wondrous Power versus the Telluric Gods in Angélica Freitas and Odyr Bernardi's *Guadalupe*

Guadalupe, by Angélica Freitas (1973–), with artwork by Odyr Bernardi, who worked on the novel *Copacabana* analyzed in chapter 7, is a feminist-queer narrative that exemplifies well the global consciousness of graphic writing in Brazil. As the title (the name of the protagonist) suggests, the narrative is set in Mexico, which is immediately confirmed by the opening full-page panel: although there is no text, anyone familiar with Mexico City immediately recognizes the iconic Palacio de Bellas Artes in the lower-left foreground and the hills ranged around the city that appear in the background. Mexico City's perpetually cloudy and smoggy sky (especially in the cooler summer months) hang low over the hills and vast reaches of a city that, despite being one of the two or three largest in the world, is characterized by a skyline with few tall buildings, even in the historical city center where the Palacio is located. Although Freitas's text is written in Portuguese, there are abundant cultural references to Mexico, including prominent features of Mexican Spanish, such as a veritable unifying presence of that quintessential Mexican food, the taco.[1]

Guadalupe (and it is important to note that the name does not occur in Brazil) is something of a contemporary Mexican feminist everywoman. Freitas captures well the strong-minded character of Mexico City women of recent generations, who are breaking very much with the model of feminine modesty and demureness that continues to be part of a more general Mexican imaginary as tied traditionally to the conventional image of the Virgen de Guadalupe, after whom Freitas's character is paradigmatically named.[2] Guadalupe is still searching for her place in life, and the narrative closes with a series of images of her fleeing her past life, journeying to places unknown in search of her own

A. Freitas and B. Odyr, *Guadalupe: uma roadtrip fantástica*

personal meaning. And while her own feminist sentiments do not apparently extend to queering amorous and erotic relationships, she is raised in a queer environment: after the unexplained disappearance of her parents, she is raised by her mother's brother, who lives his life cross-dressed as the woman Minerva.

Guadalupe only discovers this after her grandmother Elivira (Minerva's mother), who also helps raise her and with whom Guadalupe still lives as a young adult, escaped an abusive marriage in Oaxaca where violence came at the hands of her husband (her marriage was arranged). This violence stemmed from both the fact that their son identifies in a transgendered fashion as a girl and that the mother still harbors an emotional attachment to her childhood friend, Juanita, whose photograph is discovered among Elvira's personal effects. Although it appears that Elvira never had emotional entanglements with other women in Mexico City, her household enables Minerva's sexual identity, who gives up being a cabaret transvestite performer to own a bookstore in order to provide her niece with a stable economic environment. Elvira and Minerva also enable Guadalupe's rebellious nature, a reduplication of the gender rebellion and nonconformance of the two older women. Indeed, we learn early on that while Elvira was still a cabaret performer and before she became the child's surrogate mother, she would take Guadalupe with her to her dressing room, where we see Guadalupe interacting with the other transvestite performers, even helping one with her lipstick. Guadalupe enthusiastically agrees not to tell her parents where Minerva takes her, which only strengthens the sisterly bond between the young girl and her transgendered guide in what is Mexico City's extensive queer underworld—which is today more and more visible with changing sexual mores in the Mexican capital, if not in Mexican society as a whole.

The central narrative incident in Freitas's novel is Elvira's sudden death. Since she foretells to Guadalupe that it is imminent, Guadalupe and Minerva suspect that it may have been suicide, especially since she crashes the motorcycle she roars around the city on with reckless abandon into the taco stand of a man she hates. Indeed, there is a constant in *Guadalupe* of antimasculine animosity, part certainly of Elvira's lesbianism and her treatment at the hands of her father and her husband and Minerva's transgender comportment, which is an overt defiance of the heteronormative gender binary whose violence she first experienced in beatings at the hands of her father.[3]

Elvira's death immediately occasions a crisis for Guadalupe and Minerva. The woman had repeatedly emphasized her request to be buried back in her native Oaxaca, with a traditional funeral accompanied by mariachi musicians. Although Minerva originally balks at the complications involved, Guadalupe insists, and they set out on a road trip from Mexico City southeast to Oaxaca. Along the way, their bookstore delivery van breaks down and Guadalupe calls a friend of Minerva's to come and help them continue their journey to Oaxaca. This friend, Chino, who owns a repair garage, at one point self-identifies as Guadalupe's uncle, and we are led to believe that he was also once a part of the cast of performers at the Divina Perla (Divine Pearl) cabaret where Minerva was the star. And although Guadalupe identifies him with the "gay circuit," she also knows that he suffers from unrequited love for her, but she is not ready for his proposals of matrimony: less, one suspects, because of her feminist rejection of matrimony as the necessary passage in a young woman's life than for lack of any lingering attachment to conventional heteronormative matrimony. At that, Guadalupe has yet to learn of how that passage was imposed on her grandmother, not because of her lesbian relationship with Juanita, which she seems likely to have pursued after marriage, but because Elvira's father could not accept an unmarried daughter, which would socially imply that daughter's lesbianism.

All good road stories (and this one to bury Elvira in Oaxaca is but a harbinger of the one Guadalupe undertakes at the end of the novel) go nowhere narratively if there are not impediments along the way. The breakdown of the delivery van is a serious one, but much more serious is the appearance at a roadside restaurant of a mysterious and unsavory character who hypnotizes Minerva into allowing him to hitch a ride with them; when Guadalupe objects, he also gives her the evil eye and she allows him into the van. We already know who this evil agent is: he has been sent by the telluric underworld god Xyzótlan, who is in desperate need of dead souls to maintain, one supposes, his legitimacy and authority. In modern Mexico, no one believes any longer in gods like Xyzótlan (the name is invented by Freitas—note that it is based on the concluding alphabetic sequence XYZ), and this one is threatened with losing his *alvará*, something like his license or permit to continue to exist in the pantheon of Mexican telluric gods, it would appear. The allegation is made that his realm is being taken over by outside "sects."

The figures of Xyzótlan (this last of the gods because of the alphabetic configuration of his name?) and his nasty procuring agent, seeking souls for the underworld as one might pimpishly seek new workers in a brothel, clearly function here as icons of an oppressive masculinism that

A. Freitas and B. Odyr, *Guadalupe: uma roadtrip fantástica*

is still a threat to the expanding feminist-queer world the main characters of *Guadalupe* represent. Aside from any insinuation of the male-
dominated pantheon of ancient Mexican deities (which also included, to
be sure, major female figures such as the all-powerful goddess of life and
death, Coatlicue/Tonantzin), Xyzótlan unquestionably incarnates the
abiding masculinism, including still-bedrock heterosexism, of modern
Mexican society. The god is loud and violent, and he abuses his henchman both verbally and physically, demanding the fulfillment of his demands for "um corpo quente" (a warm body), which implies not just
the harvesting of dead souls, but the ritualistic manipulation of the surviving body as well.

Guadalupe, who has not been as fully dominated by the Xyzótlan's
henchman as her aunt has been (after all, each new generation, one
hopes, exercises greater feminist powers of resistance), ingests some of
her aunt's stash of hallucinogenic magic mushrooms and, in response to
the henchman's invocation of the powers of his god, she calls on the gay-
marked Village People to come to her assistance. They enter with their
theme song, "YMCA," and the henchman is quickly dispatched, changing into a bird of prey to fly, one suspects, back to his god's netherworld.

Guadalupe's transformation into a Wonder Woman heroine,[4] to com-
bat the dastardly Xyzótlan who would take possession of her grandmother's body and soul, plays out against one of the most distinctive
cultural parameters of the Oaxaca region, the phenomenon of the *muxe*.[5]
Indeed, Guadalupe's figure, transformed by the magic mushrooms, par-
odies the Marvel Comics character Wonder Woman and similar Mexican action comics by being portrayed, on the cover of a comic book
(by Mescal, rather than, Marvel, Productions), as the Muxe Maravilha,
Wonder Woman, in this pastiche of the Oaxacan word for transgendered
woman and the Portuguese word for wonder (Minerva Maravilha was,
we know from the account of her cabaret days, Minerva's stage name).
The word *muxe* is not indigenous in origin, even though the transgendered phenomenon it represents is: *muxe* is a premodern colloquial pro-
nunciation of the modern Spanish word for woman, *mujer*. The transgendered phenomenon of the *muxe* in the Oaxaca region (it is most
paradigmatically identified with the fishing village of Juchitán) is both
a gender structure parallel to the European heteronormative binary en-
forced by the Spanish conquerors and inherited by modern Mexican patriarchal society and a practice that clashes, sometimes violently, with
the heteronormativity of that patriarchal society. In the former instance,
the practice of the *muxe* is accepted—and, in some instances, even ven-

A. Freitas and B. Odyr, *Guadalupe: uma roadtrip fantástica*

erated—by the underlying indigenous society and its remnants in the region.

Yet as modernity prevails in Mexico, the practice of the *muxe* often comes to be reinterpreted as a version of a pan-Mexico and internationalist gay culture that is either vigorously opposed by conventional heteronormativity or recognized and accepted to varying degrees by the perspectives of the modern that validate alternatives to that conventional heteronormativity—that is, an expanding queer sensitivity with regard to human amorous and erotic relationships. While Mexico City is officially gay-friendly, as captured by the universe in which Guadalupe easily moves, other parts of Mexico may not necessarily be so, and underlying *muxe*-like indigenous heritage does not guarantee freedom from the sort of homophobia displayed by Elvira's husband and Minerva's father, not to mention by Elvira's father, so anxious to have her married—or so he thought—to thwart the relationship between her and Juanita.

Freitas's narrative can hardly delve with any depth into the complexities of the *muxe* phenomenon, which serves here both as a support for Guadalupe's determination, as she becomes transformed by the mushrooms into the Muxe Maravilha, to carry out her grandmother's wishes, and as a confirmation of the queer world she inhabits and here defends by complying, precisely, with those wishes. While she is not completely aware of the entire story as yet, Minerva's story about Elvira's life echoes for Guadalupe her grandmother's injunction to seek out Juanita in Oaxaca, because she would "know what to do." Thus, the final scene of Elvira's interment is Guadalupe's embrace, almost literally over her grandmother's grave, of the latter's long-lost lover.

Freitas's narrative displaces a Brazilian globalized consciousness not only in the setting in Mexico and the use of Mexican Spanish and cultural referents. Such a consciousness comes through in the joyful characterization of international feminist values, which are confirmed by Guadalupe's setting out, in the second but truncated road story of the novel, to find herself in the world.[6] It is also reinforced by the uncomplicated validation of the queer universe in which Guadalupe moves and in the reinscription of the pre-Columbian practices of *muxe* culture through the use of the magic mushrooms.[7] While all of this could have certainly been accomplished by setting the story anywhere in a multifaceted urban Brazil, and while Freitas's "displacement" to Mexico likely has little to do with educating Brazilian readers as to queer and feminist perspectives in that country, it does certainly satisfy a Brazilian interest in being internationalist and globalized in as many and varied ways as possible.

Fábio Moon and Gabriel Bá, even when writing in English directly for publication in the United States, still remain tied, in their work together, to Brazilian themes (even though both have worked with others on projects that are not thematically Brazilian). Freitas remains anchored in the Portuguese language (even though *Guadalupe* uses some Spanish), but she evidently finds it very important for her own feminist and queer consciousness to connect with stories elsewhere in Latin America.

Notes

Preface

1. Although perhaps not an issue of major theoretical importance, there is a considerable divide between those, as I do, who insist on the distinction between the comic book and graphic narrative and those who emphasize a continuity—and, therefore, the lack of a valid differentiation—between the two. Chute ("Comics as Literature?") exemplifies continuity, placing both the comic book and the graphic narrative within a large universal tradition in which image and text are correlated (what the Spanish Baroque, for example, called the *emblema* [emblem]; one also thinks of the medieval tradition of poems on the so-called "dance of death" accompanied by woodcuts). Witek, while continuing to use the term *comic book*, nevertheless focuses on the particular usefulness of the "transformation" of the comic into graphic narrative, with its expression of "sober content" for recounting historical event and process (quoted phrases taken from the back cover). Another dimension, one directly related to the relative sophistication of narrative representation (graphic and/or verbal) has to do with whether so-called comics constitute an art form worthy of serious academic attention. Beaty vigorously defends such a proposition.

2. The awarding of one of the twenty-one 2014 MacArthur Foundation Genius Grants to graphic novelist Alison Bechdel, author of the 2006 best-selling *Fun Home*, may well be considered something of a definitive establishment recognition of the graphic narrative as a unique cultural genre. The 2009 publication by the key professional organization of the Modern Language Association of the sourcebook *Teaching the Graphic Novel* is also a defining academic achievement for the recognition of the phenomenology of the genre.

3. The Library of Congress classification system has yet to catch up with the level of production, which threatens to overwhelm the scant space in the classification schedules allotted to the genre. A good argument can be made for full integration of graphic narratives into the already existing literature schedules.

4. Attention will, however, be called to the amount of Argentine material from the period of the neofascist military dictatorship (1976–1983) and the im-

mediately following period of redemocratization that was published originally in France, with extensive English translations published in the United States. Also, in the case of Brazil, attention will be called to the work of the twin brothers Fábio Moon and Gabriel Bá, who are, in addition to collaborative work with US production teams working in English, now publishing their own coauthored work in English without Brazilian translations.

5. The history of the comic book and the graphic novel in Argentina—the authors do not distinguish between the two genres—is charted masterfully by Gociol and Rosemberg; see also surveys by Accorsi and Williams.

6. Merino provides an excellent outline of the abiding importance of Oesterheld's work. Her characterization of him as the "literary voice" of Argentine comics underscores a major aspect of his work that, precisely, I would argue, serves to separate it from comics and to ground a separate cultural genre.

7. As Chute notes, "Some of the most riveting [graphic] books out there—the ones waking up literary critics—represent often vicious historical realities [and they are] particularly relevant to literary scholars because of the way they represent history through narrative" ("Comics as Literature?" 437). Additionally, "I would suggest that the compounding of word and image has led to new possibilities for writing history that combine formal experimentation with an appeal of mass readerships" (439).

8. Atencio makes this point in her recent study of cultural "reckonings with dictatorship in Brazil," which come far later in Argentina. However, my own work on Brazilian film does attempt to identify specific issues of the society of repression, through gender-marked texts, in the films of the 1980s and 1990s. Atencio makes the important point that—while Argentina named a truth commission as early as 1983, immediately after the new democratically elected president Raúl Alfonsín assumed office, which produced the best-selling report *Nunca más* in late 1984 (it has remained in print ever since)—Brazil only named a truth commission in 2011 (appointed by President Dilma Rousseff), which did not begin work until 2012 and has yet to produce any report (Atencio 17–18). Indeed the 1979 Amnesty Law and the 1995 Law of the Disappeared seem to have encouraged interest in cultural production assessing the dictatorship (Atencio 12–16).

9. One almost has the sense that the New York locale only serves to make the material more marketable in English (or French) translation, since the texture of life in Buenos Aires remains alien, one would propose, to most graphic novel readers. By contrast, Carlos Sampayo and Francisco Solano López set their *Evaristo*, which references a legendary Buenos Aires police commissioner who was active in the 1950s and early 1960s, in Buenos Aires, since the cases and police procedures presented could not simply be reset in New York or elsewhere. The English translation of *Evaristo*, however, only uses half of the original Spanish-language material, as though choosing only those stories whose context is minimally alien to foreign readers.

10. Other Latin American countries have begun to evince still rather modest inventories of graphic narrative production, and I could have doubled the size of this study by including important texts from countries like Chile, Co-

lombia, Peru, and Cuba, not to mention the significant amount of material being produced by US Latino artists (see Aldama, *Your Brain*, for Latino examples, as well as his "Mood, Mystery" on the recent texts of Gilbert Hernandez, part of the creative team known as Los Bros. Hernandez, who have an extensive production; *Redrawing the Nation* reveals material outside Argentina and Brazil that could be identified as graphic narrative). Mexico remains an anomaly. While comic-book production there reaches historic proportions, the inventory of graphic novels remains quite anemic, at least in terms of literary merit and despite good graphic innovations. Campbell addresses the continued importance of comics in dealing with current sociopolitical issues in his ¡*Viva la historieta!*, while his "Signs of Empire" surveys a more properly identified graphic narrative with a content approach that is still basically grounded in the comic book.

Chapter 1

1. Hojman Conde provides an excellent characterization of the narrative's status among Argentine readers. Pons discusses the narrative in the context of Spanish-language graphic art, with emphasis on the singular contributions of the Argentine tradition. Mazzocchi places the narrative in the context of Argentine graphic art and discusses the complexities of its history and current fame. This essay was published in a somewhat briefer version in *Transmodernity: Journal of Peripheral Cultural Production of the Luso-Hispanic World* 3.1 (2013): 22 pp. Online. Accessed January 8, 2014. http://escholarship.org/uc/ssha_transmodernity.

2. Hojman Conde asserts that "*El Eternauta* is as uniquely Argentine as *Martín Fierro*" (142). Von Sprecher provides a detailed content analysis of *El Eternauta* and select other Oesterheld texts. As Reati notes, "The Argentine comic strip came of age in the late 1950s when renowned author Héctor Germán Oesterheld chose Buenos Aires as the setting for the alien invasion that is at the center of his *El Eternauta*" (100). As I will be arguing throughout this study, it is precisely this "coming of age" that marks the transition between the low-common-denominator comic and the more subtle and sociohistorically consciousness graphic narrative that develops with Oesterheld's work as a significant precedent.

3. Trillo informs us that "[*El Eternauta* es] el único relato gráfico que es comprado por el Ministerio de Educación argentino para que no falte en las escuelas ni en las bibliotecas populares" (11). For a journalistic survey of Oesterheld's work as a whole, see Sasturain, *El aventurador*. See Sasturain, "Solano" for an account of the artistic importance of Francisco Solano López's work.

4. I am using "male narrator" and "masculinity" here in a very direct and transparent fashion that is consonant with the positive image of men in much popular culture: an uninterrogated view of male-male bonding that privileges male prerogatives while at the same time assuming men's responsibility for the sustainment of the social and economic order and the protection of hearth and home. While some graphic narrative texts may submit such an interpretation to

deconstructionist scrutiny, Oesterheld's heroic male characters, both in *El Eternauta* and his other work, are fully consonant with such a transparent definition.

5. Feinmann writes: "Juan Salvo debe abandonar el paraíso y salir al frío, al hambre, a la guerra y, por fin, al odio" ([Juan Salvo must abandon Paradise and go out into the cold, facing hunger, war and, finally, hatred] 9). By contrast with Feinmann's lost-paradise vision of *El Eternauta*, Oesterheld himself preferred to stress its Robinson Crusoe dimensions (Oesterheld–Solano López, *El Eternauta* 14). Solano López, however, notes that "La comparación con Robinson Crusoe no me convenció mucho" ([The comparison to Robinson Crusoe didn't much convince me] Oesterheld–Solano López, *El Eternauta* 15).

6. As an adjective *salvo* means "he or that which has been saved"; it is also an archaic past participle of the verb *salvar*, "saved," both in the sense of "placed out of danger" and "redeemed."

7. Fernández L'Hoeste deals specifically with Oesterheld's overarching commitment to Argentine national history in his excellent examination of Oesterheld and Leopoldo Durañona's graphic historical account, *Latinoamérica y el imperialismo: 450 años de guerra*, published in 1973–1974 in the Peronist magazine *El descamisado*.

8. One wonders if Oesterheld is conscious of honoring his German ancestors' belief that houses, especially bedrooms, must be sealed tight against noxious outside drafts.

9. As Trillo observes with reference to these historical events in the quote I have used as an epigraph to this chapter, "La inocente lectura de 1957 dejó de ser posible" (11). Feinmann elaborates on how *El Eternauta* was reread after 1976 — by implication, by those who had read it as children with the innocence Trillo remarks on.

10. This is the case with the very title of Morhain's study, which only mentions Oesterheld.

11. For a detailed account of the Proceso, see Novaro and Palermo. Rosenblatt provides a detailed analysis of the various versions of *El Eternauta*, with an important emphasis on the Solano López versus Breccia graphic aspects. There is a need for detailed analyses of the actual graphic aspects of Latin American graphic narratives, as there is a preponderance of emphasis, as in the present essay, on ideological aspects of the verbal texts.

12. There are two documentary films on Oesterheld: *H.G.O.* (1998) and *Hora cero* (2002). Vázquez discusses in detail ideological fault lines in *H.G.O.* on the basis of the intersection of biography and history.

13. Sasturain discusses in detail the ideological issues associated with Oesterheld's construction of his collective or group hero in his writing in general.

14. Hojman Conde casts Oesterheld's hero in somewhat more universal terms: "*El Eternauta* will never cease to be that myth of Man who seeks to satisfy and justify the fantasy of adventure, the search for a road to travel where the beginning point and the way back are unknown" (143–144).

15. Canaparo provides an excellent and detailed analysis of scientific and technological aspects of the narrative. The entire issue of the *Revista iberoamericana* in which it appears is devoted to Argentine science fiction.

16. Galvani studies in detail, nevertheless, the way in which the representa-

tion of violence in *El Eternauta* foreshadows Oesterheld's involvement with the Montonero movement. Pirela Sojo examines the autobiographical elements of the narrative.

17. Andrés Avellaneda examines the role of censorship in Argentina, commenting on the training of the censors in the careful interpretive reading of suspect texts. See Feitlowitz on the rhetorical strategies of the 1976–1983 dictatorship.

18. Fraser and Méndez provide a valuable characterization of the successes and limitations of the representation of Buenos Aires in *El Eternauta*.

19. There is much written about how science fiction works in societies that do not have a prominent, path-breaking scientific community like the United States or certain Western European countries (despite the fact that several Argentines are unique among Latin Americans in having won Nobel Prizes in the sciences). Ferreira provides Latin American contextualization for *El Eternauta*. Rubbione discusses Oesterheld's relationship to science fiction writing in Argentina.

20. Mike Davis speaks of the readiness with which the masters of globalization are willing to convert the so-called Third World into a "planet of slums" in order to protect their way of life. This is not fundamentally different from the north directing an atomic bomb against the south as a form of preemptive defense. One notes that the bomb is delivered by a French bombardier, which blocks Oesterheld from being accused of pandering to anti-US sentiment among the left in Argentina and the rest of South America at the time (Page comments on this point in the second, Oesterheld-Breccia, version of the story). Muñoz in his note on the history of *El Eternauta* comments briefly on how in post-Oesterheld versions of the story "los invasores se han afincado y nos dominan con el poder económico y político" ([the invaders have settled in and are controlling us with their economic and political power] 13). Morhain appears to analyze in detail the political dimensions of *El Eternauta*; however, I have not been able to consult this study. It is important to note that *El Eternauta* is one of the Argentine cultural texts that has been promoted, so to speak, by the Kirchner and Fernández de Kirchner governments. The Argentine Biblioteca Nacional held a major exhibit, a *muestra homenaje* [tribute show], in 2007 on the thirtieth anniversary of Oesterheld's disappearance and the fiftieth anniversary of the first publication of the narrative. See also the government-sponsored documentary *Hora cero* (2002). Page addresses in detail the role of popular-culture materials like *El Eternauta* in intellectual ideologies. Page provides a very persuasive argument that if *El Eternauta* is an allegory of anything, it is the crisis of intellectuals in Argentina following Peronismo (1946–1955), when intellectuals felt the need to identify—as Oesterheld himself did by joining the Montoneros— with popular revolutionaries. This proposition is certainly very much part of the sociopolitical climate of the Kirchner and Fernández de Kirchner governments. Oesterheld addresses specifically the relationship between imperialism and Latin America in the strips he published in 1973–1974 at the height of such discussions in Latin America, *Latinoamérica y el imperialismo*.

21. Germán García's standard history in the mid-twentieth century of Argentine fiction (published in 1952) mentions, and then only in the briefest fashion,

less than a dozen women novelists. The prominence of Argentine women writers today cannot obscure the fact only of few of those writing before the late twentieth century received any critical recognition.

22. Brant provides, from a queer perspective, one of the many discussions of women in Borges. Jurado, who was an intimate friend of Borges throughout his adult life, provides a more benevolent view of women in his work. Carter's note is an early entry in what will become a recurring issue in Borges criticism.

23. Whether this means that these narratives were produced exclusively with a masculine audience in mind may be questionable, but it would seem to be confirmed by the fact that the overwhelming preponderance of Latin American graphic narrative (as is also the case of the larger field of cartoon art) is drawn by men. Foster, in his study of Latin American graphic humor (*From Mafalda*), examines the work of only one woman artist among a dozen practitioners studied. She is Patricia Breccia, the daughter of Alberto Breccia. Of the twenty-one Latino graphic artists interviewed by Aldama, only two are women. Incidentally, the cover image of Aldama's book is from Trillo's *Chicanos* series in English, drawn by Eduardo Risso.

24. All of the latter were notorious for the secondary and subservient role of women, although the presence of women was, in fact, notable when one considers how their direct aggressors, the Argentine Armed Forces, constituted, at the time, a strictly male society. Certain women did become guerrilla leaders, such as the notorious Norma Arostito of the Montoneros.

25. Although Solano López is mostly consistent in representing the *tú* form graphically with its corresponding verbal forms, he does slip up on one occasion, when Martita tells her father "¡Tocá el chichón! ([Feel this bump!] 312), referring to an accidental bump on her neck she has received. Perhaps the "mistake" is in Oesterheld's narrative and Solano López simply copied it verbatim, with no second thought, into his panel. Oesterheld, in the conventional narrative publication of his stories, retains the *tú* form, while the sequel by Solano López and Maiztegui (the reversal of names that puts that of the graphic artist first is due to Solano López's greater reputation) employs the Argentine *voseo*.

26. Which is, indeed, the case with some of the non-Argentine editions of Quino's strip, and I suspect it is true with some of the video versions as well. International editions of Argentine graphic materials customarily involve such a grammatical modification.

27. The *vos* form exists elsewhere in Latin America, but always within a particular set of national sociolinguistic coordinates. On the geographic extension of the *voseo* in Latin America, see Rona; on the affirmation of the *voseo* in Argentine literature, see Gregorio de Mac. Ernesto Sábato published his important existential novel *El túnel* in 1948 using the so-called universal *tú* form, despite its being set in Buenos Aires; in 1966 he rewrote it substituting the Argentine *vos* (Foster, "Tú y vos").

28. Oesterheld wrote many other action stories with non-Argentine characters, where it is reasonable that they would not speak with the *tú* form. On another note, in *El Eternauta*, the *usted* is used far more than it would be today. For example, Franco addresses Salvo and Favalli using the *usted* form, and Salvo's truco partners use the *usted* form with his wife, Elena. Today in these two sociolinguistic contexts, the *vos* would most likely be used.

29. Typical here would be the four-and-a-half-hour-long documentary film *La hora de los hornos* (1968; dir. Octavio Getino and Fernando Solanas).

30. One might argue that I am overlooking Evita Perón here, but it is not hard to argue that her brief direct participation in Argentine politics (from the assumption of power by her husband Juan Domingo Perón in 1946 to her early death from cancer in 1952) meant essentially her manipulation, with very, very few possible exceptions, of the dynamics of masculine power. It is a moot question as to whether, had she lived longer, she might have actualized a feminine power base.

Chapter 2

1. Sinner is a former New York policeman turned private detective. The framework of his stories, as established in the first volume, is to retell his experiences as both policeman and detective, in Joe's Bar. Sinner leaves the police force (and is effectively shoved out) because he is unable to collaborate with its death-squad mentality in which the force effectively places itself, with the acquiescence of society, above the law.

2. There is a real Joe's Bar in New York City, which probably should not be surprising, given the rather generic name; see Westhoff (84).

3. *El Bar de Joe* is remarkably accurate in its depiction of New York City, including the abundant use of English as part of the cityscape. There is only one error of detail, and that is when Joe, on his way home in the early hours of the morning, is stopped by the police, who demand to see his identity papers. Americans, of course, do not have, and therefore do not carry, identity papers. Even if, in the past decade because of the hysteria over so-called illegals, America has converted the state driver's license into an ersatz identity document (many states require proof of citizenship in order to obtain one), this would not have been the case in the 1980s. And perhaps not even today would someone like Joe, in New York City, even have a driver's license.

4. In the case of Cortázar's story, which comes from the collection *Las armas secretas* (1959), the hidden event is discovered to be the sexual seduction of a young boy. In Michelangelo Antonioni's film version, *Blow-Up* (1966), it is a murder. In both cases, the photographer is devastated by his inability to alter an event that has already taken place, where art has distanced him from reality rather than providing a privileged approximation. Unlike a chance bystander on the street, he can do nothing to either identify the perpetrator or his victim, as all he has at hand is the deferred sign of his photograph. José Muñoz published in 2009 an illustrated edition of Cortázar's famous story "El perseguidor" [The pursuer] also from *Las armas secretas* [Secret weapons]. "El perseguidor" is based loosely on the career of Charlie Parker.

5. As Argentines, Muñoz and Sampayo would both be familiar with the tango lyrics by Enrique Santos Discépolo and music by Mariano Mores, "Cafetín de Buenos Aires," where the narrator-singer describes becoming a man by hanging out with men in a Buenos Aires bar (text in Albuquerque 8). See my analysis of the tango in Foster, *Buenos Aires* (65–69). See also Bossio on Buenos Aires bar culture. Gociol and Rosemberg include Muñoz and Sampayo in their study

of the Argentine comic strip, despite their extensive work outside Argentina and the fact that Sampayo writes in French. They quote fellow comic-book scholar Pablo De Santis to the effect that the duo's work on non-Argentine themes, such as that set in New York, is far better than their attempts to return to national subjects (277). I would agree, since their graphic novel on Gardel is not stellar work (on the other hand, it does have the merit of raising the issue of Gardel's supposed sexual ambiguity); bibliographic information would indicate that *Carlos Gardel: la voz del Río de la Plata* was written first in Spanish and then first published in French translation. On the other hand, the collection of narratives *Evaristo: Deep City*, devoted to prizefighter-turned-police-commissioner Evaristo (no other name given) is a superbly worked text. This is some of Muñoz's and Sampayo's best collaborate work and, in narrative situations and tone, their most Argentine.

6. For a discussion of New York lesbian bars, see Faderman.

7. The comparison with Buenos Aires is a bit complicated, since bars in Argentina often function also as restaurants and are interchangeably called "cafés." Young people may also freely enter, with few restrictions, bars in Buenos Aires. Indeed, students may often study alone or in groups in neighborhood bars, where a coffee or a Coke will usually get you unlimited table time. Cocktail lounges, especially connected to hotels, may function in Buenos Aires in a fashion more closely paralleling New York, including the presence of upscale prostitutes.

8. There is surprisingly very little research on New York bars. See Stott's encyclopedia entry, where he observes that by "the mid-1990s the neighborhood bar was an endangered institution in many parts of the city and especially in Manhattan, largely because the income it generated was not commensurate with the high cost of real estate" (80).

9. As in the case of the now widely-commented-on Vivian Maier (1926–2009), a Chicago nanny who took something like one hundred thousand photographs on the streets of Chicago and environs, which she hoarded in storage lockers without ever publishing or even sharing a single one with anyone else. See John Maloof and Charlie Siskel's documentary, *Finding Vivian Maier* (2013).

10. [Photographs from a year-and-a-half of personal life. Photographs in which she doesn't appear even once, as if the ephemeral nature of the mirror were enough: it restores her image while always hiding it because it is not reflected.]

11. [I want to take advantage of the light for taking photographs. I want to be alone to think about you and remember you.]

12. It is at this point, after she leaves the doctor to take her camera back to the early-morning streets, that she comes upon the police scene involving Pepe's dead body. This intersection of the two stories, however, involves a narrative error: we see Pepe's eyeglasses on the pavement alongside him (91), while in the earlier story the woman who picks him up has broken them as part of the rage in which she destroys the photograph of Pepe with his parents and attempts to rip up his passport; throughout the rest of the story, Pepe is without glasses. There is also a narrative intersection with the story "Willcox & Conrad" involving a hired killer.

13. In a nicely passing visual touch, the image of the two men walking away holding hands also contains a jet plane flying over, as though foreshadowing her flight occasioned by the relationship between the two men.

14. Perhaps Vivian Maier intuited this in her refusal ever to share her images with anyone.

Chapter 3

1. This is an interesting translation problem. "Piloto" in Argentine Spanish means both pilot and raincoat (I suppose a metonymy is involved here: it's the type of raincoat worn by pilots). Since the graphic image is of someone wearing a raincoat, I opt to translate it with that word.

2. I have been unable to establish a useful bibliographic account of the pre-book distribution of the stories. Gociol and Rosemberg note that the chapters of the first story, *El piloto del olvido*, appeared in Buenos Aires in the vanguard illustrated magazine *Fierro* beginning in July 1985 (446–447). As a consequence of publication in Spain, *Perramus* exhibits the customary imperative that Peninsular lexical and grammatical norms be adhered to. Therefore, the Argentine *vos* is replaced by *tú*, along with the plural form *vosotros*, which is rather jarring because the strip is so anchored in Argentine sociohistorical factors. This is even more so in the case of the gallery of socially marginal types reminiscent of the novels of Roberto Arlt that appear in *El alma de la ciudad*, the second story of the first volume.

3. The first *Perramus* volume garnered an Amnesty International Human Rights Prize in 1988 for its representation of repressive military tyranny.

4. Chandler's full characterization is "Down these mean streets a man must go who is not himself mean, who is neither tarnished nor afraid. . . . He is the hero, he is everything. He must be a complete man and a common man and yet an unusual man. He must be, to use a rather weathered phrase, a man of honor, by instinct, by inevitability, without thought of it, and certainly without saying it. He must be the best man in his world and a good enough man for any world" (991–992). Lest one find it inappropriate to characterize Perramus in terms of a character from American popular fiction, it is important to recognize the enormous influence of—and homage to—American popular culture in Argentine comics and graphic narratives, as seen in the names of numerous characters created by Breccia and associates. Concomitant with such influence is the presence of New York, as I have commented on in my discussion of Juan Sampayo and Antonio Muñoz's work.

5. Ferman provides an extensive commentary on the importance of Borges in what she calls a "relato policial" ([police story] 138–144). One will recall that Borges, in addition to reworking detective-novel motifs in his fiction, was a constant champion of traditional, especially Anglo-American, forms of that genre.

6. As Gociol and Rosemberg observe, "La elección [de Borges] no es arbitraria: la culpa, el olvido, el tiempo, la memoria . . . Son todas figuras borgeanas. Pero hay algo más, los autores no reconstruyen el Borges que fue sino el que ellos—y muchos argentinos progresistas—hubieran deseado que fuera: una figura sin fisuras ideológicas. Por eso, en la ficción, el gran escritor participa de la

resistencia" ([The choice of Borges is not arbitrary: guilt, oblivion, time, memory . . . These are Borgean figures. Moreover, the authors do not reconstruct the Borges that was, but rather the Borges that they—and many progressive Argentines—would have wanted him to be: a figure without ideological fissures. That's why in the story the great writer is a part of the resistance] 448).

7. Perramus and his sidekicks identify as members of the guerrilla group VVV (Vanguardia Voluntarista para la Victoria [Volunteer Vanguard for Victory]). This name is a riff on the state-sponsored terror group created in the mid-1970s even before the 1976 military coup, the nefarious AAA (Asociación Anticomunista Argentina [Argentine Anticommunist Association], also called the Triple-A).

8. As mentioned, the title of the story contains a play on words. The word *piloto* in Argentine Spanish has the basic meaning, common to all dialects of the language, of "pilot." However, in Argentina, a *piloto* is a raincoat, and the gift of the item of clothing from the prostitute then becomes an icon of as much the circumstances of his loss of identity, his descent into oblivion, as it is of his ascent out of it in the (re)construction of his identity as a man of heroic principle.

9. There is no comprehensive examination of the relationship between Borges and Buenos Aires, although it is evident from his first published book, the poetry that makes up *Fervor de Buenos Aires* (1923). There is a volume in English that brings together a solid array of his poetry, fictional texts, and essays related to Buenos Aires and Argentina (Borges, *On Argentina*).

10. This is a slightly misquoted verse (it actually reads "La ciudad, ahora, es como un plano / De mis humillaciones y fracasos" [The city is now like a map / Of my humiliations and failures]; from the poem "Buenos Aires" in Borges's collection *El otro, el mismo* ([The one, the same] 1964) included in his *Obras completas* (947).

11. There are extensive Jewish elements in Borges's writing, as Edna Aizenberg has demonstrated, not just references and allusions, but elements essential to plot construction, as in this case.

12. Of course, I am using the Augustinian binary here. But the truth is that, aside from a bevy of madams and prostitutes, Breccia and Sasturain's Buenos Aires is a totally masculinist space. From one point of view, this could be explained on the basis of the way in which repressive tyranny is at the hands of the masculinist armed forces. Yet the analogy between the masculinist armed forces and the inherent sexism of the narrative—as is the case with Latin American graphic narrative in general—is not insignificant.

Chapter 4

1. Chandler's famous detective character Philip Marlowe is specifically mentioned by Pablo De Santis in his prefatory note to the Spanish edition of *Evaristo* (9).

2. Published in English as *Evaristo: Deep City* (1986). The English version only includes six of the original thirteen stories in Spanish. The original 1985 book publication was in French as *La Mort est toujours au rendez-vous*, and it ap-

pears that *Evaristo* was not published in book form in Spanish in Argentina until 1998. The strips appeared originally in the cultural journal *Fierro* in 1985. *Fierro* was one of the most important cultural publications of that period, which involved the return to constitutional democracy in Argentina beginning in late 1983. See Ferman 92–105. *Fierro*, which appeared between 1984 and 1987, was directed by Juan Sasturain. De Santis places *Fierro* in the context of similar cultural magazines.

3. One understands Evaristo to be the police commissioner's last name. Although Evaristo is a common first name in Spanish, it can also be an Italo-Argentine last name. It is common practice in Argentina for people to be addressed directly by their last name without accompanying honorifics and to be referred to in the same fashion by strangers (such as when Evaristo is pointed out on the street); it is not, therefore, surprising that we never learn his first name, not even when he registers as a guest in a provincial hotel. The back cover, however, of the original Spanish edition asserts that Sampayo and Solano López's character is based on a legendary commissary by the name of Evaristo Meneses (1907–1992), so the reader can choose between the first name of the historical figure and the last name of Argentine sociolinguistic usage. Biographical information on Evaristo Meneses is provided by Juan Pablo Meneses, "Los códigos de Meneses"; see also "Evaristo Meneses." Meneses after his retirement published in 1964 a personal memoir of his police work. He notes that at the time, Buenos Aires was made up of fifty police commissaries (Meneses 127). None of the cases presented in Sampayo and Solano López's graphic narrative appear to be drawn from Meneses's memoir.

4. Translations are from *Evaristo: Deep City.*

5. One of the most notable accounts of the matter, Pearlman's *The Capture of Adolf Eichmann*, gives short shrift to the very existence of Argentina, although it does detail the diplomatic crisis the capture occasioned between the two countries. Perhaps a certain disdain for Argentina is part of the sordid story of how Perón's government provided a safe haven for Eichmann, Joseph Mengele (the so-called Dr. Death), and thousands of other Nazis and Nazi sympathizers.

6. Note again the implied anti-Semitic tone of the editor's name (Peres is the Sephardic equivalent of Pérez), present in the mealy-mouthed nature of the Jewish doctor (Lubitsch) whose daughter has disappeared in this story ("El célebre caso Lubitsch" [The famous Lubitsch case]), the victim of Pérez-Peres's attentions, or in the story about the secret foreign agents ("Operación Hermann" [The Hermann operation]—Hermann is a German name, presumably that of the Eichmann-like character; Herman would be the Yiddish/Jewish equivalent), in which the infiltrated agents are abetted by powerful local Jewish interests, which we are meant to identify as such because of stereotypical physical characteristics and a prominently displayed menorah. I am making no claims about anti-Semitism for either Solano López or Sampayo, but rather am noting the verisimilitude of the pervasive anti-Semitism in the Argentina of the period (see the extensive and detailed study by Senkman on the anti-Semitism in Argentina).

7. One could attribute muckraking and other yellow journalism practices to *La Razón*. Yet for many it provided, at least until the period of the 1976–1983 neofascist tyranny, which contributed to its eventual disappearance from the Ar-

gentine journalist scene, a reliable and impartial coverage of the news. One sur-mises that it was likely too "impartial" for those with interests identified with the radical left.

8. One could add to this also profoundly homophobic, although none of the material in *Evaristo* points to the urban reality of so-called sexual deviation, de-spite its historically high incidence in Buenos Aires.

Chapter 5

1. Gociol and Rosemberg discuss the role of "Las mujeres," Ch. 5 (216–254). This essay originally appeared in *Ámbitos feministas* 14 (2014): 61–74.

2. Ferman offers an extensive analysis of the postmodern feminist elements in Breccia's work, emphasizing the expressionistic elements of her artwork (194–209), something like a profound graphic revisionism of masculinist realism. Fer-man identifies the artist as Patricia Brescia rather than Breccia. Breccia was the only woman to draw for the important cultural review *Fierro* (1984–1987). Yet women in the United States and Europe have been solidly associated with the graphic narrative, and Chute's *Graphic Women*, in addition to surveying US feminist examples, argues for how important autobiographical comics by women have been in the twenty-first century, with texts by Marjane Satrapi and Alison Bechdel being prime examples.

3. She published her graphic humor under the name only of Maitena, but her conventional narrative fiction has been published with her full name.

4. She is also the sister of graphic artists Enrique Breccia (1946–) and Cris-tina Breccia (1951–).

5. The importance of *Humor registrado* and the other two magazines is char-acterized by Gociol and Rosemberg (52–55), who call them "El último refugio" [The last refuge]. They mention the contributions of Alberto, Enrique, and Pa-tricia to the three publications.

6. I examine *Sol de Noche* in detail in my *From Mafalda to Los Supermachos* (65–73). See also the brief commentary by Gociol and Rosemberg (251–252).

7. Breccia's personal website is titled "Salvajeando" [Going savage] a most apt characterization of her scathing artistic language.

8. Although the name Breccia used without a first name is understood in Ar-gentine cultural history to refer to Alberto Breccia, I will be using it throughout the rest of this essay to refer to Patricia Breccia.

9. I am engaging in some revised self-plagiarism here, having used the same reference to Merecader's novel and Scalabrini Ortiz's essay in my discussion of Sylvina Frydlewsy's photography in my *Argentine, Mexican, and Guatemalan Photography* (47–61).

10. Although not published as a collected volume until 1999, the stories of *Sin novedad* were composed in the first half of the 1980s.

11. Many of Breccia's narratives are set at night, thereby making the moon an ever-present detail of the urban landscape. The name Sol de Noche is derived from the Argentine brand name of a kerosene lantern, much like the American Coleman lantern. Just as women cannot compete on the male landscape, the kerosene lantern is no match for the man-made illumination of the cityscape.

12. The Spanish title is, to be sure, *Sin novedad en el frente* (1929; trans. Eduardo Foertsch and Benjamín Jarnés). There is also a 1978 retranslation by Manuel Serrat.

13. Gociol and Rosemberg provide a brief characterization of *Sin novedad en el frente* (252–53): "Todo en la historieta, parece desbordarse" ([Everything in the strip seems to overflow] 253).

14. [Four in the morning, the hour when the angels tell small stories of bedeviled love . . . / . . . a dark hour when foolish women take to flying out the windows . . . / . . . and when certain hearts leak like broken pipes.]

15. Such an image is an interesting characterization of the possible masturbatory context of such anonymous calls.

16. The incomplete use of the exclamation mark in both utterances (the opening one in that of the moon; the closing one in that of the serpent) is characteristic of Breccia's graphic/orthographic anomalies.

17. [. . . But in reality . . . Nothing is going on, only the howl of the train, the moon keeping an eye on a couple of things, the intact plaza beneath the startled lamp lights . . . Or the sound of a cat walking in a low voice.]

18. In the panel in which we see the woman examining the scene below on the sidewalk from her apartment balcony, the bracelet is on her left wrist, as it is in some previous panels, but these are obviously narrative errors of no consequence.

19. *Sin novedad* became the center of a controversy of censorship in Mendoza in mid-2013. Copies of it were included in a shipment of material distributed free of charge to school programs by the national Ministerio de Educación. Although drawn in the early 1980s, not published until 1999, Breccia's material was still provocative enough in 2013 to be officially banned by local authorities (Kenis). It must be noted that one dimension of the controversy concerns relations between the parameters of the metropolitan culture of Buenos Aires and those of the diverse Argentine provinces.

Chapter 6

1. The fact that the original Portuguese-language edition has an English title establishes immediately how important English is for this postmodern, globalized Brazilian graphic narrative production.

2. Since this is a Brazilian graphic novel and since Brazilians do not shy away from sex, even the most circumstantial representation of it, in the way in which American artists might, the Devil portrays prominently his primary sexual attributes.

3. Brazil is a country that moves by an excellent network of cross-country highways, both for general transportation (cars, trucks, and often quite upscale passenger buses, all of which depend on an overlying network of sometimes quite elaborate truck stops). The road functions as a powerful metaphor in the culture of a country the size of the United States, as is to be seen in the title of one of its great novels, João Guimarães Rosa's *Grandes sertões: veredas* (1956). The official English-language title is *The Devil to Pay in the Backlands*, but the literal translation of the title is "Great Backlands: Tracks," where "tracks" refers

to paths or roads through the backlands, which are, in turn, a metaphor for the vastness of Brazilian geography. A more recent example of the road metaphor in Brazilian literature is Paulo Thiago's film *Jorge, um brasileiro* (1989), where Jorge is an Everyman icon and his road trip recounted in the film an allegory of Brazilian social life in the context of the country's return to democracy in 1985. One will note the use of the definite article in the title, reinforcing the iconic nature of this one man. I analyze this film in my *Gender and Society* (18–27).

4. Here we have what one might call the Superman matrix present in a film nevertheless colored by leftist concepts of human solidarity, when one customarily associates the Superman-like figure with the reactionary individualism of the American ur-text.

5. It is not uncommon for commercial Brazilian to use key business terms drawn from English.

6. Sangrecco's one claim to fame is that he believes he's an Elvis Presley impersonator far better than Elvis himself. He quotes Presley's song "A Little Less Conversation" as he slaughters people, lamenting that his audiences never survive to applaud him.

7. As opposed to those written directly in English, such as the most recent work of Fábio Moon and Gabriel Bá that I analyze elsewhere in this study.

Chapter 7

1. This chapter was originally published in *Critical Insights: Magical Realism*, 131–145, edited by Ignacio López-Calvo (Ipswich, MA: Salem Press; Grey House Publishing, 2014).

2. "Highly textured in its narrative scaffolding, comics [i.e., graphic narrative] doesn't [*sic*] blend the visual and the verbal—or use one simply to illustrate the other—but is rather prone to present the two nonsynchronically; a reader of comics not only fills in the gaps between panels but also works with the often disjunctive back-and-forth *reading* and *looking* for meaning" (Chute 452).

3. Galera is well established as an important writer of vanguard narratives, which will alert the reader to the so-called high literary contexts for *Cachalote*. Coutinho is the son of the legendary cartoonist Laerte Coutinho, who signs his work with only his first name.

4. There is no pagination in this volume, a frequent occurrence in graphic narratives.

5. The scientific facts relating to beached whales are taken from the "Beached Whale" entry in *Wikipedia*, accessed November 11, 2013.

6. By this time, the reader will have realized that Galera and Coutinho's narrative necessarily evokes the most famous symbolic whale in Western literature, Herman Melville's novel, *Moby Dick* (1851). Melville's whale is steeped in multiple symbolic meanings, befitting the sort of symbolist narrative of the time, and interpretations of the white whale range across multiple interpretational nodes. Yet no matter how many multiple interpretations are associated with Moby Dick, there is little question that Melville means for his reader to see him as a *symbol* of something, something that must be viewed with a deep resonance in the narrative texture of the novel. The reader of *Cachalote* is left to wonder

what degree of resonances this white whale might have. For an example of recent critical analysis of the figure of the whale in *Moby Dick*, see Calkins; see Bouk and Burnett for the importance of leviathans in the nineteenth-century imaginary.

7. As a consequence, one presumes, of the inclusion of the practice of kinbaku in *Cachalote*, my copy, purchased in the São Paulo Livraria Cultura in July 2010, comes with the front cover sticker "Só para adultos!" [For adults only!]—although one wonders if the exclamation mark means that the sticker is more of a tease come-on than a warning. Kinbaku is like other select Japanese erotic practices, such as deep punishment enemas or the representation of sexual activities in the 1976 Japanese film *In the Realm of the Senses*, directed by Nagisa Oshima. At least in terms of what is available on the Internet, all of this material is masculinist-anchored, with or without willing female sexual partners. I have found the scantest of references to trussed males and no trace of female-male or same-sex variations. Let me make it clear I am referring to kinbaku, which is specifically identified in the Galera-Coutinho text, not to other sexualized forms of bodily immobilization. Sadomasochism in Hispanic literature does not yet have much of a bibliography, with the exception of the Argentine Alejandra Pizarnik's lesbian-marked *La condesa sangrienta* (1971) and *Fe en disfraz* (2009) by the Puerto Rican author Mayra Santos-Febres. See the discussion of the sources for Santos-Febres's novel by Arce.

8. Interestingly enough, as another dimension of underdeveloped narrative schemata in *Cachalote*, there is a physical resemblance between Vitório and the little boy at the end of the novel. And at one point, Vitório and Lara end up swimming together in a pool at someone's house party, although they discover no white whale in the pool. Later they will swim together in the stormy ocean, and Vitório will rescue Lara from drowning as he leans down and picks her up as he rides an imposing black steed, enacting a medieval fantasy of chivalric manhood. But again, no white whale appears.

9. This image, in a light salmon color in place of white and a burnt sienna in place of black, now serves to illustrate the cover of editions of *Cachalote* subsequent to the first one.

10. I examine the relationship of Brazilian culture to what was a more Spanish-language production, the *nueva narrativa hispanoamericana* [New Spanish-American narrative] or the boom in Foster, "Brazil and the Boom." Yet, while not exactly chronologically coterminous with Spanish-language production, Brazil does evince an equivalent experimental production, and certainly something as "magically realist" as the Spanish-American paradigms.

11. Volek is not the first to use this term (it is customarily attributed to the Chilean scholar José Joaquín Brunner), but Volek can be credited with having discussed the issue at length.

Chapter 8

1. Some of the many literary interpretations of Copacabana are found in Coutinho and Machado. O'Donnell provides a fascinating history of the development of Copacabana as a residential and then as a commercial and tour-

ist district. Coutinho and Machado speak of the "myth" and of an eternal city, as though, like Rome, Copacabana were an imperial city in its own right. O'Donnell speaks of the "invention" of Copacabana. For the sort of typical photobook on Rio as tourist mecca that I claim *Copacabana* has as an intertextual reference, see Donner. Lobo and Odyr's book has a fairly large presence on the Internet as Latin American photo books go.

2. Odyr Bernardi prefers to be known simply as Odyr. It is common practice in Brazil for individuals to be known only by their first name and, indeed, for artists and personalities to be identified only by their first name. Thus, Pres. Dilma Rousseff is identified universally simply as Dilma.

3. Several online commentaries have commented on the noir aspect of *Copacabana*; one of the better commentaries is by Andrade, reproduced from the magazine *Revista o grito!*

4. The Lobo–Odyr narrative is mentioned in Blanchette's analysis of sexual tourism in Copacabana (83–84). The novel is signed only with Sandro Lobo's last name and Odyr Bernardi's first name.

5. One scene does involve a text message received by cell phone (81). Since it involves an exchange between Diana and Suelen regarding the setup of the Gringo, supposedly both have cell phones, but they do not recur again in the story.

6. It is important to note here that adult prostitution, with respect to both sexes, is not illegal in Brazil, although brothels and pimping (which today customarily involves the larger issue of human trafficking) are. Child prostitution is a particular problem in Brazil, although Lobo and Odyr do not address it in their novel. It is naïve, however, to view the legality of prostitution as creating an idyllic realm of uncompromised "sex work," since all range of activities associated with it (i.e., physical abuse, drugs, theft, extortion/badgering, and the virtual imprisonment of prostitutes) falls within the dynamics of the trade, not to mention the routine exploitation of underage individuals. A comprehensive view of Brazilian street prostitution, based on oral histories, is provided by Olivar. Green has much to say about prostitution in Rio de Janeiro in his book on homosexuality in Brazil.

7. Diana literally does a balance sheet in her head of her transactions in order to make sure she meets the rent, fulfills her mother's demands, and, presumably, other costs of her trade, such as what her pimp will demand and what articles of the profession she must purchase. In one panel, an interior monologue about finally having found an interesting man, the four words of the monologue in Portuguese are distributed over four frames in which we see Diana, in rapid succession, with four different men.

8. In turn, cunnilingus is preferred by many of the women when they are seeking sex from their boyfriends, and cunnilingus appears to be the sexual act Suelen would wish to perform on Diana when she briefly invokes the frequent lesbianism between prostitutes: she uses the vulgar Brazilian metaphor for sex in general, *comer* (to eat), which most figuratively implies oral sex (65).

9. Before Diana and her boyfriend are "saved" by the retired general's dagger cane, the detective in the employ of the Gringo whom Suelen and Diana have robbed is going to turn Diana's boyfriend over to his associate for sodom-

izing unless she reveals the whereabouts of the money; the associate affirms himself eager to play his part (176).

10. Brazilians showed, through the height of the AIDS pandemic, marked unwillingness to practice safe sex. Since the pandemic has been brought under control in Brazil thanks to the AIDS cocktail, there is even greater reluctance, at least among the general populace, to practice safe sex.

11. Albeit the film takes place in the Los Angeles Chinatown, not in the legendary San Francisco one.

Chapter 9

1. Anyone who has worked with comics and graphic narratives knows how difficult it is to exercise full bibliographic control over the various instantiations of a particular text or series, as much of it does not get formally cataloged, and the Library of Congress Cataloging-in-Publication information, now standard in conventional print publishing, does not customarily appear in these imprints. As of this writing (October 2013), *Daytripper* is listed in the OCLC WorldCat as held by over eight hundred libraries, the vast majority of them US public libraries.

2. Bá's name shows up as illustrator of Maff Fraction's *Casanova* series (2011–) and Gerard Way's *The Umbrella Academy* series (2008–). However, both Bá and Moon appear as illustrators of Mike Mignola's *B.P.R.D. Vampire* series (2011–).

Chapter 10

1. At one point, Freitas shows Minerva (who is, of course, speaking in Spanish, although we are reading her translated, so to speak, into Portuguese) combining the two languages. The balloon representing her speech combines a Mexican-Spanish phatic interjection with a comment in response to something her interlocutor has said with a phrase in Portuguese: "Orale, que surpresa" ([Wow, what a surprise] no pag.).

2. There is much historical and ideological bibliography on the Virgen de Guadalupe, including discussions of her feminist and even lesbian dimensions. One excellent source is Gaspar de Alba's analysis of the artwork on the Virgen by Alma López.

3. The latter at one point, belt in hand, shouts "¡Cabrón!" in the face of the mother who is shielding her son from the man's anger. The reader is left to wonder whether this all-purpose Mexican insult (something like the American "motherfucker"), used here in the masculine form, is directed against his wife, whom he probably knows to have had a lesbian relationship with Juanita and whom he, to be sure, faults for their son's gender nonconformance, or against the son, whom he therefore forcefully identifies as masculine, despite the young child's female clothing and feminine earring. (One notes that in using this Spanish interjection, Freitas is attentive to the use of the introductory inverted exclamation mark Spanish, but not Portuguese, makes use of.)

4. Freitas's use of the Wonder Woman icon is an important index of the shift from comics to graphic narrative, in that it involves a specific feminist attribution to the figure that is difficult to extract from representation at the level of the comic book. The relationship that Marshall establishes between the Wonder Woman figure and the classical Furies involves resonances of some level of cultural sophistication that one might expect to encounter in the graphic novel but not in the frequently shoddy cultural perspectives of the comics. Yet, having made that distinction, I must acknowledge that Marshall's essay appears in a book that belongs to the practice of eschewing a distinction between the comics and graphic narrative.

5. There is much anthropological work on the *muxe*, which refers to men who cross-gender as women; *nguiu* is the term for the less-common phenomenon of women who cross-dress as men. For a recent anthropological study, see Miano Borruso. One of the most important records of gender in Oaxaca is the photography of Graciela Iturbide, with texts by the novelist Elena Poniatowska. Foster examines the gender issues in Iturbide's photographs. It is important to note that, while the Oaxacan phenomenon of the *muxe* is alluded to by Freitas, neither Elvira nor Juanita engage in cross-gendering, making them more consonant with lesbian identity than with the *muxe* phenomenon. In addition to the more frequent *muxe*, *muxé* is also used; this latter form replicates the stress pattern of the modern word *mujer*.

6. Xyzótlan's henchman, in a bid for his freedom after having been subdued by the Village People, offers Minerva a mirror of gods, in which one can see oneself twenty years hence. Minerva offers it to Guadalupe, who sees herself as an old maid now in charge of Minerva's bookstore. As she sets out on her own personal adventure, she will throw the magic mirror overboard from a boat on which she is escaping her past and, by implication, her grimly foretold future. It goes without saying that it is to the masculinist gods' advantage for women to look into their future and see themselves as shriveled creatures.

7. It is of little consequence that the ritualistic consumption of hallucinogenic mushrooms by indigenous groups is not coextensive with the phenomenon of the *muxe*. Their intersection here must be taken as a fictional license, as one does of the nonexistent figure of Xyzótlan.

Works Cited

Accorsi, Andrés. "Argentine Comics." *International Journal of Comic Art* 3.2 (2001): 23–43.

Aizenberg, Edna. "'I, a Jew': Borges, Nazism, and the Shoah." *The Jewish Quarterly Review* 104.3 (2014): 339–353.

Albuquerque, M. A. *Antología de tangos.* 8th ed. Mexico City: Medina, 1970.

Aldama, Frederick Luis. "Mood, Mystery, and Demystification in Gilbert Hernandez's Twenty-First-Century NeoNoir Stand-Alones." *Image TexT: Interdisciplinary Comics Studies* 7.1 (2013). Accessed December 27, 2013. The entire journal is devoted to the Los Bros. Hernandez creative team.

———. *Your Brain on Latino Comics: From Gus Arriola to Los Bros. Hernandez.* Austin: University of Texas Press, 2009.

Andrade, Lidianne. "Copabana [*sic*] em versão noir e cruel." *Revista o Grito!* (June 22, 2009). Accessed January 29, 2014.

Antonioni, Michelangelo, dir. *Blow-Up.* United Kingdom: Bridge Films; Carlo Ponti Productions; MGM, 1966.

Arce, Chrissy B. "La fe disfrazada y la complicidad del deseo." In *Lección errante: Mayra Santos-Febres y el Caribe contemporáneo,* edited by Nadia V. Celis and Juan Pablo Rivera, 226–246. San Juan, Puerto Rico: Isla Negra Editorial, 2011.

Argentina. Biblioteca Nacional. *H.G.O. + El Eternauta. Muestra homenaje.* Buenos Aires, 2007. Exhibit brochure.

Atencio, Rebecca J. *Memory's Turn: Reckoning with Dictatorship in Brazil.* Madison: University of Wisconsin Press, 2014.

Avellaneda, Andrés. *Censura, autoritarismo y cultura: Argentina 1960–1983.* Buenos Aires: Centro Editor de América Latina, 1986.

Balbo, Víctor, and Daniel Stefanello, dirs. *H.G.O. (Héctor Germán Oesterheld): nos contó infinidad de historias . . . ahora debemos contar la suya.* Argentina. Buenos Aires Autoren. 1998. 145 min.

Barthes, Roland. *S/Z.* Translated by Richard Miller, with a preface by Richard Howard. 1st American ed. New York: Hill and Wang, 1974.

"Beached Whale" (now "Cetacean Stranding"). *Wikipedia.* Accessed November 11, 2013.

Beaty, Bart. *Comics versus Art.* Toronto: University of Toronto Press, 2012.

Bechdel, Alison. *Fun Home: A Family Tragicomedy.* Boston: Houghton Mifflin, 2009.

Berone, Lucas. "Memoria y figuraciones del futuro, en *El Eternauta* de H. G. Oesterheld." In *Actas del VII Congreso Internacional Orbis Tertius de Teoría y Crítica Literaria, mayo 18–20, 2009*, edited by Sergio Pastorelmo. La Plata: Universidad Nacional de La Plata, Facultad de Humanidades y Ciencias de la Educación, 2011. Accessed August 26, 2013.

Blanchette, Thaddeus Gregory. "'Fariseos' e 'gringos bons': masculinidade e turismo sexual em Copacabana." In *Gênero, sexo, amor e dinheiro: mobilidades transnacionais envolvendo o Brasil*, 57–102, edited by Adriana Piscetelli et al. Campinas, Brazil: UNICAMP/PAGU, 2001.

Borges, Jorge Luis. "La muerte y la brújula." 1942. In his *Obras completas*, 499–507. Buenos Aires: Emecé Editores, 1974.

———. *Obras completas.* Buenos Aires: Emecé Editores, 1974.

———. *On Argentina.* Edited and with an introduction and notes by Alfred MacAdam. New York: Penguin Books, 2010.

Bossio, Jorge Alberto. *Los cafés de Buenos Aires.* Buenos Aires: Editorial Schapire, 1968.

Bouk, Dan, and D. Graham Burnett. "Knowledge of the Leviathan: Charles W. Morgan Anatomizes His Whale." *Journal of the Early Republic* 28.3 (2008): 433–466.

Brant, Herbert J. "The Queer Use of Communal Women in Borges' 'El muerto' and 'La intrusa.'" *Hispanófila* 125 (1999): 37–50.

Breccia, Alberto, and Juan Sasturain. *Perramus.* 1st ed. in Spanish. Prologue by Osvaldo Soriano. Barcelona: Editorial Lumen; Buenos Aires: Ediciones de la Flor, Ediciones Culturales Argentinas, 1987. Orig. published in French, Grenoble: Glénat, 1986.

———. *Perramus: diente por diente.* Buenos Aires: Ediciones de la Flor, 2006.

———. *Perramus: la isla de guano.* Barcelona: Ediciones B, 1993.

Breccia, Patricia. *Sin novedad en el frente.* Buenos Aires: Ediciones Colihue, 1999.

Breckenridge, Janis. "Tracing (Argentine) Feminism across Time, or How Maitena Plays with *La histori(et)a*." *Chasqui: revista de literatura latinoamericana* 45.1 (November 2016), 42–53.

Calkins, Jennifer. "How Is It Then with the Whale? Using Scientific Data to Explore Textual Embodiment." *Configurations* 18.1 (2010): 31–47.

Campbell, Bruce. "Signs of Empire in Mexican Graphic Narrative: A Research Agenda." In *Spanish and Empire*, edited by Nelsy Echávez-Solano and Kenya C. Dworkin y Méndez, 173–196. Nashville: Vanderbilt University Press, 2007.

———. *¡Viva la historieta! Mexican Comics, NAFTA, and the Politics of Globalization.* Jackson: University Press of Mississippi, 2009.

Canaparo, Claudio. "*Mobilis in mobili*: ciencia y tecnología en *El Eternauta*." *Revista iberoamericana* 221 (October–December 2007): 871–886.

Cancio, José Luis, dir. *Hora cero: un documental sobre Héctor Germán Oesterheld.* Argentina: La Pintada Producciones, 2002.

Carter, E. D., Jr. "Women in the Short Stories of Jorge Luis Borges." *Pacific Coast Philology* 14 (October 1979): 13–19.

Chandler, Raymond. "The Simple Art of Murder." In his *Later Novels and Other Writings*, 977–992. New York: Library of America, 1995.

Chute, Hillary. "Comics as Literature? Reading Graphic Narrative." *PMLA* 123.2 (2008): 452–465.

———. *Graphic Women: Life Narrative & Contemporary Comics*. New York: Columbia University Press, 2010.

Cortázar, Julio. *Las armas secretas*. Buenos Aires: Editorial Sudamericana, 1959.

———. *El perseguidor*. Ilustraciones de José Muñoz. Barcelona: Libros del Zorro Rojo, 2009.

———. *Rayuela*. Buenos Aires: Editorial Sudamericana, 1963.

Coutinho, Wilson. "Introdução." In *Copacabana: cidade eterna: 100 anos de um mito*, edited by Wilson Coutinho and Aníbal Machado, 9–13. Rio de Janeiro: Relume Dumará, 1992.

Coutinho, Wilson, and Aníbal Machado, eds. *Copacabana: cidade eterna: 100 anos de um mito*. Rio de Janeiro: Relume Dumará, 1992.

Davis, Mike. *Planet of Slums*. London: Verso, 2006.

De Santis, Pablo. "El comisario y el león." In *Evaristo*, by Carlos Sampayo and Francisco Solano López, 9–10. Buenos Aires: Ediciones Colihue, 1998.

———. "The *Fierro* Years: An Exercise in Melancholy." In *Redrawing the Nation: National Identity in Latin/o American Comics*, edited by Héctor Fernández L'Hoeste and Juan Poblete, 191–203. New York: Palgrave Macmillan, 2009.

Deleuze, Gilles. *Cinema*. Translated by Hugh Tomlinson and Barbara Habberjam. Minneapolis: University of Minnesota Press, 1986–1989.

Deleuze, Gilles, and Félix Guattari. *A Thousand Plateaus: Capitalism and Schizophrenia*. Translated by Brian Massumi. London: Continuum, 2004.

Donner, Hans, Felix Richter, and Martin Fiegl. *Rio de Janeiro*. Rio de Janeiro: Céu Azul de Copacabana Editora, 2003.

"Evaristo Meneses, un comisario que se conviritó en leyenda." Internet. Accessed October 23, 2014.

Faderman, Lillian. *Odd Girls and Twilight Lovers: A History of Lesbian Life in Twentieth-Century America*. New York: Columbia University Press, 1991.

Feinmann, José Pablo. "Crónica desde los límites del terror." In Héctor Germán Oesterheld y Francisco Solano López, *El Eternauta II*, 8–18. Buenos Aires: Biblioteca Clarín de la Historieta, 2004.

Feitlowitz, Marguerite. *A Lexicon of Terror: Argentina and the Legacies of Torture*. Oxford: Oxford University Press, 1998.

Ferman, Claudia. *Política y posmodernidad: hacia una lectura de la antimodernidad en América Latina*. Miami: Iberian Studies Institute, North-South Center, University of Miami, 1993.

Fernández L'Hoeste, Héctor. "Del nacionalismo como treta de la imaginación identitaria en *450 años de guerra contra el imperialismo*, de Héctor Germán Oesterheld and Leopoldo Durañona." *Revista iberoamericana* 77.234 (2011): 41–57.

Fernández L'Hoeste, Héctor, and Juan Poblete. *Redrawing the Nation: National Identity in Latin/o American Comics*. New York: Palgrave Macmillan, 2009.

Ferreira, Rachel Haywood. "Más allá, *El Eternauta*, and the Dawn of the

Golden Age of Latin American Science Fiction (1953–59)." *Extrapolation* 51.2 (2010): 281–303.

Foster, David William. "Adolfo Prieto: Profile of a Parricidal Literary Critic." *Latin American Research Review* 13.3 (1978): 125–145.

———. *Argentine, Mexican, and Guatemalan Photography: Feminist, Queer, and Post-Masculinist Perspectives.* Austin: University of Texas Press, 2014.

———. "Brazil and the Boom." In *Teaching the Latin American Boom*, edited by Lucile Kerr and Alejandro Herrer-Olaizola, 137–146. New York: Modern Language Association of America, 2015.

———. *Buenos Aires: Perspectives on the City and Cultural Production.* Gainesville: University Press of Florida, 1998.

———. "Drawing São Paulo: The Graphic Fiction of Fábio Moon and Gabriel Bá." In his *São Paulo: Perspectives on the City and Cultural Production*, 135–150. Gainesville: University Press of Florida, 2011. Orig. *Ciberletras* 19 (July 2008): 14 pages. http://www.lehman.edu/ciberletras/v19/foster.html.

———. "Fontanarrosa's *Gauchomania* and *Gauchophobia* in *Las aventuras de Inodoro Pereyra*." In his *From Mafalda to Los supermachos*, 37–51. Boulder, CO: Lynne Rienner, 1989.

———. *From Mafalda to Los supermachos: Latin American Graphic Humor.* Boulder, CO: Lynne Rienner, 1989.

———. *Gender and Society in Contemporary Brazilian Cinema.* Austin: University of Texas Press, 1999.

———. "Masculinity as Privileged Human Agency in H. S. Oesterheld's *El Eternauta*." *Transmodernity: Journal of Peripheral Cultural Production of the Luso-Hispanic World* 3.1 (2013): 22 pp. Online. Accessed January 8, 2014. http://escholarship.org/uc/ssha_transmodernity.

———. "News Bulletins from the Gender Wars: Patricia Breccia's *Sin novedad en el frente*." *Ámbitos feministas* 14 (2014): 61–74.

———. "Queering Gender in Graciela Iturbide's Juchitán de las mujeres." In his *Argentine, Mexican, and Guatemalan Photography: Feminist, Queer, and Post-Masculinist Perspectives*, 90–105. Austin: University of Texas Press, 2014.

———. "Tú y vos en *El túnel* de Ernesto Sábato." *Hispania* 54 (1971): 354–355.

———. "The Unbearable Weight of Being in Daniel Galera and Rafael Coutinho's *Cachalote*." In *Critical Insights: Magical Realism*, edited by Ignacio López-Calvo, 131–145. Amenia, NY: Salem Press, Grey House Publishing, 2014.

Foster, David William, and Roberto Reis, eds. *Bodies and Biases: Sexualities in Hispanic Cultures and Literatures.* Minneapolis: University of Minnesota Press, 1996.

Foucault, Michel. "Of Other Spaces, Heterotopias." *Architecture, Mouvement, Continuité* 5 (1984): 46–49. French and English translations online: http://foucault.info/documents/heterotopia/foucault.heterotopia.en.html. Accessed May 28, 2014.

Fraser, Benjamin, and Claudia Méndez. "Espacio, tiempo, ciudad: la representación de Buenos Aires en *El Eternauta* (1957–1959) de Héctor Germán Oesterheld." *Revista iberoamericana* 238–239 (January–June 2012): 57–72.

Freitas, Angélica, and Odyr Bernardi. *Guadalupe: uma roadtrip fantástica.* São Paulo: Companhia das Letras, 2012.

Fuentes, Carlos. *La nueva novela hispanoamericana*. Mexico City: Joaquín Mortiz, 1969.

Galera, Daniel, and Rafael Coutinho. *Cachalote*. São Paulo: Quadrinhos na Cia, 2010.

Galvani, Iván. "*El Eternauta* como representación de la masacre: acerca del carácter real de las representaciones." *Revista question* 20 (Spring 2008). Online: Accessed August 29, 2013.

García, Germán. *La novela argentina*. Buenos Aires: Editorial Sudamericana, 1952.

Gaspar de Alba, Alicia. *Our Lady of Controversy: Alma López's "Irreverent Apparition."* Austin: University of Texas Press, 2011.

Geirola, Gustavo. "Eroticism and Homoeroticism in *Martín Fierro*." In *Bodies and Biases: Sexualities in Hispanic Cultures and Literatures*, edited by David William Foster and Roberto Reis, 246–273. Minneapolis: University of Minnesota Press, 1996.

Getino, Octavio, and Fernando Solanas, dirs. *La hora de los hornos*. Argentina, 1968.

Gociol, Judith, and Diego Rosemberg. *La historieta argentina: una historia*. Buenos Aires: Ediciones de la Flor, 2000.

González, José Eduardo. *Borges and the Politics of Form*. New York: Garland Publishing, 1998.

Grampá, Rafael. *Mesmo Delivery*. Rio de Janeiro: Desiderata, 2008.

Grampá, Rafael. *Mesmo Delivery*. Translated by Julio Mairena. Colors by Rafael Grampá and Marcus Penna. Letters by Rafa Coutinho. Milwaukie, OR: Dark Horse Books, 2014.

Green, James N. *Beyond Carnival: Male Homosexuality in Twentieth-Century Brazil*. Chicago: University of Chicago Press, 1999.

Gregorio de Mac, María Isabel de. *El voseo en la literatura argentina*. Santa Fe, Arg.: Universidad Nacional del Litoral, Facultad de Filosofía y Letras, 1967.

Hojman Conde, Claudia S. "Héctor G. Oesterheld." In *Latin American Science Fiction Writers: An A-to-Z Guide*, edited by Darrell B. Lockhart, 140–146. Westport, CT: Greenwood Press, 2004.

Iturbide, Graciela, and Elena Poniatowska. *Juchitán de las mujeres, 1979–1998*. Mexico City: Amigos de Editorial Calamus; Consejo Nacional de Bellas Artes y Literatura; Instituto Nacional de Bellas Artes y Literatura, 2010. There are various other editions of this material.

Jurado, Alicia. "La mujer en la literatura de Borges." *Boletín de la Academia Argentina de Letras* 64.253–54 (1999): 409–423.

Kenis, Diego. "Sin novedad en el frente." *Agencia Paco Urondo. Suplemento cultura popular* (September 7, 2013). Online. Accessed December 12, 2013.

Kovacs, George, and C. W. Marshall, eds. *Classics and Comics*. Oxford: Oxford University Press, 2011.

Lobo, Sandro, and Odyr Bernardi. *Copacabana*. Rio de Janeiro: Desiderata, 2009. Authors' names appear on cover as Lobo [and] Odyr.

López-Calvo, Ignacio, ed. *Critical Insights: Magical Realism*. Amenia, NY: Salem Press, Grey House Publishing, 2014.

Mallea, Eduardo. *Todo verdor perecerá*. Buenos Aires: Espasa-Calpe Argentina, 1941.

Maloof, John, and Charlie Siskel, dirs. *Finding Vivian Maier*. US: Ravine Pictures, 2013.

Marshall, C. W. "The Furies, Wonder Woman, and Dream." In *Classics and Comics*, edited by George Kovacs and C. W. Marshall, 89–101. Oxford: Oxford University Press, 2011.

Mazzocchi, Mirta Paola. "Oesterheld y la gran aventura de la historieta argentina." In *El viaje y la aventura*, edited by Gabriella Bianco and Luigi Volta, 297–307. Buenos Aires: Instituto Italiano de Cultura/Alitaria; Ediciones Corregidor, 1992.

Meneses, Evaristo. *Meneses contra el hampa: relatos policiales*. Buenos Aires: Editorial "Mam," 1964.

Meneses, Juan Pablo. "Los códigos de Meneses. Crónicas argentinas." *Clarín* .com (October 26, 2009). Internet. Accessed October 23, 2014.

Mercader, Martha. *Solamente ella*. Buenos Aires: Editorial Bruguera, 1981.

Merino, Ana. "Oesterheld, the Literary Voice of Argentine Comics." *International Journal of Comic Art* 3.2 (2001): 56–69.

Miano Borruso, Marianella. *Hombre, mujer y muxé en el Istmo de Tehuantepec*. Mexico City: Plaza y Valdés, 2002.

Mignola, Mike. *B.P.R.D.* Milwaukie, OR: Dark Horse Books, 2011–. Individual titles for volumes in the series.

Moon, Fábio, and Gabriel Bá. *Daytripper*. With coloring by Dave Stewart, lettering by Sean Konot. New York: DC Comics, 2011.

———. *Daytripper*. Tradução Érico Assis. Barueri, SP: Penini Books, 2011.

———. *De Tales: Stories from Urban Brazil*. Milwaukie, OR: Dark Horse Books, 2006.

Moore, Alan. *Watchmen*. Illustrated and lettered by Dave Gibbons, colored by John Higgins. New York: DC Comics, 1983.

Morhain, Jorge Claudio. *La Argentina premonitoria en El Eternauta de Héctor Germán Oesterheld*. Buenos Aires: Axxón 96, 1999.

Muñoz, José, and Carlos Sampayo. *Billie Holiday*. Original in French. Paris: Casterman, 1991.

———. *Billie Holiday*. Translated by Katy MacRae, Robert Boyd, Kim Thompson. Afterword by Stanley Crouch. Seattle: Fantagraphics Books, 1993.

———. *Billie Holiday*. Translated into Spanish. Barcelona: Planeta-DeAgostini, 2005.

———. *Carlos Gardel: la voz del Río de la Plata*. Barcelona: Libros del Zorro Rojo, 2010.

———. *Carlos Gardel: la voix de l'Argentine*. Translated by Dominique Grange. Paris: Fallimard, 2007.

———. *El Bar de Joe*. Translated by Diego de los Santos. Barcelona: Planeta-DeAgostini, 2005. Vol. 1 of *Historias del bar*.

———. *Joe's Bar*. Translator unknown. New York: Catalan Communications, 1987.

———. *Le Bar à Joe*. Paris: Casterman, 1981.

———. *Skinner*. Translated by Deborah Bonner. Seattle: Fantagraphic Books, 1987. Vol. 1, no. 1: "Talking with Joe."

Muñoz, Pablo. "Un poco de historia." In Héctor Germán Oesterheld and Francisco Solano López, *El Eternauta*, 12–13. Buenos Aires: Biblioteca Clarín de la Historieta, 2004.

Novaro, Marcos, and Vicente Palermo. *Historia argentina: la dictadura militar 1976–1983, del golpe de estado a la restauración democrática*. Buenos Aires: Paidós, 2003.

O'Donnell, Julie. *A invenção de Copacabana: culturas urbanas e estilos de vida no Rio de Janeiro (1890–1940)*. Rio de Janeiro: Zahar, 2013.

Oesterheld, Héctor Germán. *El Eternauta y otros cuentos de ciencia ficción*. Buenos Aires: Ediciones Colihue, 1996.

Oesterheld, Héctor Germán, and Alfredo Breccia. *El Eternauta*. Buenos Aires: Ediciones de la Urraca, 1982.

Oesterheld, Héctor Germán, Alfredo Breccia, and Enrique Breccia. *Evita* (Oesterheld and A. Breccia]/*El Che* [Oesterheld and A. and E. Breccia]). Buenos Aires: Nueva Biblioteca Clarín de la Historieta, 2007.

Oesterheld, Héctor Germán, and Leopoldo Durañona. *Latinoamérica y el imperialismo: 450 años de guerra*. Buenos Aires: Doeyo y Viniega Editores, 2004.

Oesterheld, Héctor Germán, and Francisco Solano López. *El Eternauta*. Prólogo de Carlos Trillo. Barcelona: Norma Editorial, 2008.

Olivar, José Miguel Nieto. *Devir puta: políticas da prostituição de rua na experiência de quatro mulheres militantes*. Rio de Janeiro: EdUERJ, 2013.

Oshima, Nagisa (director). *In the Realm of the Senses*. Japan: Argos Films; Oshima Productions; Shibata Organisation, 1976.

Page, Joanna. "Intellectuals, Revolution and Popular Culture: A New Reading of *El Eternauta*." *Journal of Latin American Cultural Studies* 19.1 (2010): 45–62.

Paley Francescato, Martha. "The New Man (But Not the New Woman)." In *The Final Island*, edited by Jaime Alazraki and Ivar Ivask, 134–139. Norman: University of Oklahoma Press, 1981.

Pearlman, Moshe. *The Capture of Adolf Eichmann*. London: Weidenfeld and Nicolson, 1961.

Pérez-Sánchez, Gema. "El humorismo gráfico de Maitena Burundarena: de lo local a lo global; de los estereotipos a la subversión." *Revista iberoamericana* 234 (January–March 2011): 87–110.

Pirela Sojo, Fanny. "Héctor, Germán, Oesterheld: la inscripción autobiográfica como *manifiesto* en *El Eternauta*." In *Actas digitales del Primer Congreso Internacional de Historietas*, edited by Laura Vázquez. Buenos Aires: Editorial Viñetas Serias, 2010. Online: Accessed August 28, 2013.

Polanski, Roman, dir. *Chinatown*. US: Paramount Pictures, 1974.

Pons, Álvaro. "Claves argentinas en la madurez de la historieta española: de *Rico tipo* al *Eternauta*." *Revista iberoamericana* 234 (January–March 2011): 21–40.

Prieto, Adolfo. *Borges y la nueva generación*. Buenos Aires: Letras Universitarias, 1954.

Reati, Fernando. "Argentina's Montoneros: Comics, Cartoons, and Images as Political Propaganda in the Underground Guerrilla Press of the 1970s." In *Redrawing the Nation: National Identity in Latin/o American Comics*, edited by Héctor Fernández L'Hoeste and Juan Poblete, 97–110. New York: Palgrave Macmillan, 2009.

Rommens, Aarnoud, "Memory in Camouflage: Alberto Breccia and Guillermo Saccomanno's 'William Wilson' as Catalyst for Memory." *Poetics Today* 26.2 (2005): 305–47.

Rona, José Pedro. *Geografía y morfología del "voseo."* Pórto Alegre: Pontifícia Universidade Católica do Rio Grande do Sul, 1967.

Rosa, José Gumarães. *Grande sertão: veredas.* Rio de Janeiro: J. Olympio, 1956.

Rosenblatt, Adam. "The Making and Remaking of *El Eternauta.*" *International Journal of Comic Art* 9.2 (2007): 81–92.

Rubbione, Alfredo V. E. "H. G. Oesterheld. Géneros erráticos y avatares de la ficción." In *Primeras Jornadas Internacionales de Literatura Argentina / Comparatística, Actas*, 229–234. Buenos Aires: Facultad de Filosofía y Letras, Universidad de Buenos Aires, 1995.

Ruscha, Edward. *Twenty-Six Gasoline Stations.* Alhambra, CA: Cunningham Press, 1962, c. 1969.

Sampayo, Carlos, and Francisco Solano López. *Evaristo.* Buenos Aires: Ediciones Colihue, 1998.

———. *Evaristo: Deep City.* Translated by Jeff Lisle. New York: Catalan Communications, 1986.

———. *La Mort est toujours au rendez-vous.* Paris: Dargaud, 1985.

Sasturain, Juan. *El aventurador: una lectura de Oesterheld.* Buenos Aires: Aquilina, 2010.

———. "Oesterheld y el héroe nuevo." In his *El domicilio de la aventura*, 103–126. Buenos Aires: Ediciones Colihue, 1995.

———. "Solano, el que dibujó el mito." In his *Buscando vivos*, 119–128. Buenos Aires: Astralib, Colectiva Editora, 2004.

Satrapi, Marjane. *Persepolis.* New York: Pantheon Books, 2003.

Scalabrini Ortiz, Raúl. *El hombre que está solo y espera.* Buenos Aires: Gleizer, 1931.

Senkman, Leonardo. *El antisemitismo en la Argentina.* Buenos Aires: Centro Editor de América Latina, 1986.

Solano López, Francisco, and Pablo Maiztegui. *El Eternauta: El regreso. La búsqueda de Elena.* Buenos Aires: Solano Ediciones, 2007. Cover note reads "Además: *Marcianeros* de Oesterheld y Solano."

Spiegelman, Art. *Maus: A Survivor's Tale.* New York: Pantheon Books, 1986.

Stott, Richard. "Bars, Taverns, and Saloons." In *Encyclopedia of New York*, edited by Kenneth T. Jackson, 79–80. New Haven: Yale University Press; New York: The New York Historical Society, 1995.

Tabachnick, Stephen E., ed. *Teaching the Graphic Novel.* New York: Modern Language Association of America, 2009.

Thiago, Paulo, dir. *Jorge, um brasileiro.* Brazil: Embrafilme, 1988.

Tompkins, Cynthia M. "Las mujeres alteradas y superadas de Maitena Burundarena: feminismo *Made in Argentina.*" *Studies in Latin American Popular Culture* 22 (2003): 35–60.

Trillo, Carlos, "Las muchas lecturas de un clásico." Prologue in *El Eternauta* by Héctor Germán Oesterheld and Francisco Solano López, 7–12. Barcelona:

Norma Editorial, 2008. Also 8–11 in Héctor Germán Oesterheld and Francisco Solano López, *El Eternauta*. Buenos Aires: Biblioteca Clarín de la Historieta, 2004.

Vázquez Hutnik, Laura. "30 años sin Oesterheld: alcances y límites del registro documental." *Revista question* 16 (Spring 2007). Online: Accessed August 26, 2013.

Volek, Emil. "Introduction: Changing Reality, Changing Paradigm: Who Is Afraid of Postmodernity?" In his *Latin America Writes Back: Postmodernity in the Periphery*, xi–xxviii. New York: Routledge, 2002.

Von Sprecher, Roberto. *El Eternauta: la sociedad como imposible: modelos de sociedad en las obras de Héctor Germán Oesterheld*. Córdoba, Argentina: JCV Editorial, 1998.

Weegee. *Naked City*. 1945. New York: Da Capo Press, 1985.

Westhoff, Ben. *New York City's Best Dive Bars: Drinking and Diving in the Big Apple*. Brooklyn, NY: Ig Publishing, 2010.

Williams, Jeff. "Argentine Comics Today: A Foreigner's Perspective." *International Journal of Comic Art* 3.2 (2001): 44–55.

Winogrand, Garry. *Garry Winogrand*. Edited by Leo Rubinfien. San Francisco: San Francisco Museum of Modern Art in collaboration with Yale University Press, 2013.

Witek, Joseph. *Comic Books as History: The Narrative Art of Jack Jackson, Art Spiegelman, and Harvey Pekar*. Jackson: University Press of Mississippi, 1989.

Yovanovich, Gordana. "The Role of Women in Julio Cortázar's *Rayuela*." *Revista canadiense de estudios hispánicos* 14.3 (1990): 541–552.

Index